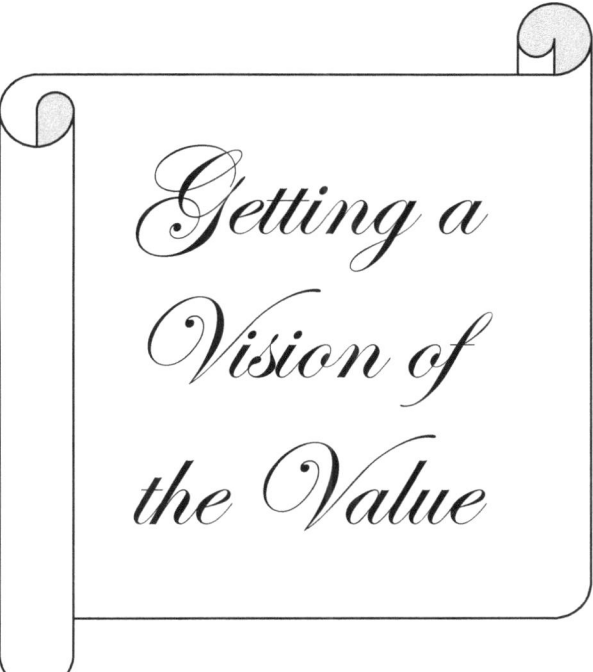

Getting a Vision of the Value

Written by Darold Edwards

Copyright © 2008 Darold F. Edwards
Editing Assistance by MyKeyWeb.com

Getting a Vision of the Value

Table of Contents:

i.	Introduction	5
ii.	Acknowledgements	15
iii.	Preface	19
I.	Getting a Vision of the Value	25
II.	The Standard	35
III.	Essentials	51
IV.	Way, Truth, Life	57
V.	Rightly Dividing the Word of Truth	63
VI.	Set in His Ways	75
VII.	The Enemy Within	81
VIII.	Boondoggles	93
IX.	Pandemic	109
X.	Life	117
XI.	Ingredients	125

NOTES

i.   A General Introduction to
The Works of

Darold Edwards

I would like to begin this introduction of myself and my writings with a greeting to all who are gracious enough to take the time to read my writings and join me in this journey of Bible exploration and study. This greeting is found in **[2 Peter 1: 2], "Grace and peace be multiplied to you through the knowledge of God, and of Jesus our Lord".** In **[Galatians 2: 6] Paul writes of people "who added nothing to me".** It is my desire and prayer that these writings will add much to you in your Bible explorations and enrichment of life.

Let me introduce myself to you. It is very likely you have never heard of me but that is alright, as I have never heard of the vast majority of you, but, I know you are out there somewhere in our big wide world that seems to be getting smaller with a disturbing amount of consistency. At the present time I am 75 years old, and like most of everything else in this world, my age is subject to constant change. My wife of 52, going on 53 years of marriage, Patricia, is a very wonderful person who has had the grace to put up with me these many years gone by and has been a constant source of help, strength, and encouragement to me; with a little challenge thrown in from time to time to help keep life interesting. But having no complaints, I am looking forward to a continuation of our life together, at least for some time to come. We have our home in Albany, Oregon, raised 3 children there and have grandchildren and great grandchildren.

After a privileged time as a child and young person under the care and guidance of some very wonderful loving parents, I proceeded on to adulthood with an average course of life doing some things I should and some that I shouldn't. My specific vocation, after various jobs, was about 42 years as an electrician which was enjoyed very much. In the latter portion of this time I was able and blessed to assist in many church construction jobs as an electrician. There came a time, however, that my body convinced me it was time to seek other easier things to do. After that career ran its course and was fading into the sunset, I was led into an interest in writing, which is where I am today and will probably be for the remainder of my time on this earth. I am enjoying it with much satisfaction, and what you see here is among the beginnings of it. I hope you will blessed by it.

My main interest and priority is and has been in pursuit of Biblical study and knowledge for several years. As I get an ever increasing **"Vision of the Value"** of such study and exploration, the interest and priority increases accordingly. This Biblical knowledge with its provision of life and life more abundantly through Jesus Christ our Lord, indeed has become my life with its great and perfect peace with joy unspeakable and full of glory. What a blessed state of being to enjoy an unending hope and blessed assurance of a future that extends from today on to and including eternity.

Not being very impressed with humanity in its general condition and what it has done to this world God has provided for it, much of my writings will be addressing this issue and whose responsible for such a degraded condition as this world is in, including our "Land of the Free and the Home of the Brave. You may not agree with me in some of my views and interpretations, but it is only important that you be in agreement with Jesus. Some of the positions I take on traditional Bible interpretations will be somewhat controversial, maybe even viewed as heretical by some, but will certainly provide reason for some new exploration of thinking and thought. God tells us in **[Isaiah 55: 8-9], "My thoughts are not your thoughts,**

neither are my ways your ways, saith the Lord. For as the heavens are higher than the earth, so are my ways higher than your ways, and my thoughts than your thoughts".

So as we re-explore some of these old traditional truths and absolutes of God's Word that have brought life, strength, stability, and comfort to all who embrace them, lets keep our minds open to other additional concepts, original ideas, thoughts and ways that are a part of the expanse between where we are today and where God is calling us to be. I do not believe, that in the fullness of God's greatness, man has reached the end of all God has for us to think about either in the knowledge we are to gain or in the development of our mental capabilities. Much education and knowledge lay before us yet to be attained to. Once again, it is not important that you agree with me, but don't get caught in disagreement with God and his Word, that is a fatal mistake that is much to prevalent in our world today.

My writings are not meant to be entertaining, though a bit of mirth from time to time is acceptable. Yet encouragement and inspiration for meditation and diligent, committed study for spiritual growth and development resulting in intimate fellowship and relationship with God and our Saviour and Lord Jesus Christ is, and remains, the priority. I will be using some words that may offend some but are meant to describe some very apparent conditions that are alive, but seemingly more sick than well, yet thriving and somewhat destructive, in humanity. God is much more of a gentleman than I am and limits his language to words such as fool, fools, and foolishness. I get a little rougher in my references to mankind and use words such as stupid, idiotic, ignorance etc.

Please understand I have nothing against people, only against the conditions listed above, stupidity, idiocy, and ignorance, etc, that humanity has such an overwhelming desire to wallow and remain in to the degradation of themselves, their societies, and nations, when God, in his love, has given us the remedy for deliverance from such nonsense. To refuse, or neglect, to avail oneself of what God has made available for deliverance from sin and its results in itself, puts a persons intelligence in question.

You are certainly welcome to disagree with me and raise an argument in protest if you wish, however, just a little understanding of the condition our nation is in and how it arrived at this state of demise from the abominations of sin and iniquity of its inhabitants should settle the argument and any questions about it once and for all.

I do hope to wake many minds that have gone to sleep to the challenge of some new in-depth thought that will project them into new ways of life and living where **"the heart is diligently kept, clean, and guarded" [Proverbs 4:23], the mind and spirit are renewed, [Romans 12: 2; Psalms 51:10], and the soul prospers" [3 John: 2].** If we continue to think the way we've always thought, we'll continue to get what we've always got. The way humanity is digressing, we cannot afford to continue along that road of demented mentality, either as individuals or as a nation.

It is my intention that other books will be written as the inspiration to do so presents itself. Several others are already in the works, all dealing with Biblical truths as they relate to the problems and dilemmas of our present day and time; all based on man's disobedience and rebellion against God. This has been the story down through the ages and has only intensified as the population of man has increased, **[Hosea 4: 7], "As they were increased, so they sinned against me: therefore I will change their glory into shame"**. It is this increase in intensity of disobedience, rebellion, sin, iniquity, etc, etc, call it what you will, that has proven so disastrous to mankind, that prompts referral to the conditions of stupidity, idiocy, and ignorance with which man has so chosen to characterize himself.

It is the overabundance of these things that has brought such confusion and chaos to our nation and indeed the world. We could work our way through some of it, but when it became the norm of mankind's mentality and conduct, we have become overwhelmed by it, and can no longer see a light at the end of the tunnel, so to speak. The problems have not changed thru the ages, but remain internal, in the mentalities of some of **"our own countrymen"** who have formed alliances against the Bible, its teachings, and those who teach it. As a result, our leaders are frustrated, the news media is frustrated, and consequently the people are driven to frustration, and confusion seems to reign supreme, especially in the ranks of the people who have rejected God's word of truth and absolutes.

I will refrain from opening any argument as to whether or not the redeemed community of Christ are any better than the unsaved, as **[John 3: 16]** points out that Christ died for all, of which we were all qualified as ungodly, **[Romans 3: 23], " For all have sinned and come short of the glory of God"**. I am willing to leave that distinction between the saved and unsaved up to God as he separates the sheep from the goats, as who qualifies as a sheep versus a goat is entirely up to him, **[Matthew 25: 32]**. In the meantime, however we might consider **[Acts 10: 34-35]** as a point of interest and consideration by those who have eyes to see, ears to hear, and minds that are capable of comprehension and at least a little bit of understanding; **"Then Peter open his mouth and said, of a truth I perceive that God is no respecter of persons: BUT in every nation he that feareth him, and worketh righteousness, is accepted with him"**.

Having favor with God through meeting his Biblical directed requirements for such favor, and being accepted with him is a very comforting, and intelligent, position to be in. You may well get away with disagreeing with me, but to disagree with God will have some eternal devastating affects: I would suggest a path more in line with God's choosing. I would offer **[Deuteronomy 30: 19]** for intense consideration and study for beginners and as a refresher for the more advanced students, or just readers, of the bible.

Please don't get me wrong: I am not down on America, only the stupidity and ignorance that is bringing about her ruin, and the idiots that promote and practice it; which is all within their "rights" of course. God created us to be intelligent beings, however, Adam cast that aside when he abdicated his dominion authority to Satan in the Garden of Eden, and man has been abdicating every since. Retained and exercised Godly intelligence would prevent the things that are bringing ruination, shame, and disgrace on our beloved America, but Godly intelligence and common sense seem to be non-existent in our nation these days along with other things mentioned in the Bible that are commensurate with righteous and holiness.

The question of, who is to blame, should prompt some interesting discussion and dialogue. Who knows, during the process, we might even discover the solution to many of our problems. As Christians, that should already be quite apparent. **[Isaiah 5: 24], "Therefore as the fire devoureth the stubble, and the flame consumeth the chaff, so their root shall be as rottenness, and their flower shall go up as the dust: BECAUSE they have cast away the law of the Lord of hosts, and despised the word of the Holy One of Israel".** The first portion of this scripture gives us a fair description of America if we don't get our spiritual act together. The latter portion gives us the result of excommunicating God and His Word by such things as "the separation of the church and state".

Then we have the remedy, **[Mark 1: 15], "Repent and believe the gospel unto diligent obedience.** This is a repeat of **[2 Chronicles 7: 14], "If my people, which are called by my name, shall humble themselves, and pray, and seek my face, and turn from their wicked ways;** *then* **I will hear from heaven, and will forgive their sin, and will heal their land".** There are a few more words used to emphasize this repentance essential, but the message is the same. **[Deuteronomy 28]** gives a very graphic difference between the people who dwell on the **"If thou wilt hearken diligently"** side of God's directions versus the unrepentant, **"If thou wilt not hearken diligently"** side in rebellion and disobedience. Consider this carefully.

Lacking the extended education that many of today's authors have, you may find my writings a bit rough around the edges for which I make no apology. This could prove an advantage in some ways as I don't have some things to unlearn as I progress and move ahead in my own studies. However, if we all stay with the same Bible for the purpose of unity, **[John 17],** and, to put in today's vernacular, "being on the same page", worshipping and serving the same God, creator of heaven and earth, the God of Israel, and diligently adhering to His counsel, we should remain fairly accurate as we progress, **"seated together in heavenly places in Christ", [Ephesians 2: 4-10],** continuing toward our eternal destiny of the kingdom of heaven while **[Deuteronomy 28: 47], "serving the Lord our God with joyfulness, and with gladness of heart for the abundance of all things".**

Though it seems that I may ramble a bit from time to time, it is my intention, whether I succeed or not, to present the readers with some Biblical truths and challenges they can get their "spiritual teeth into" for the purpose of growth, and development that they can apply toward Christian maturity, providing they are interested in doing so. If they are not so inclined, it is my prayer that some of these writings will induce enough curiosity to provide a challenge to compel them to additional studies, with my own writings and a multitude of others that are available to them. Let me challenge you to choose the books you read, and study, with wisdom and discretion, selecting only those that **"add something to you"** in the way of developing a Biblical, Christ like character, personality and attitude, **"with the Word of God dwelling in you richly", [Colossians 3: 15-17], vs. 16.**

You may find an occasional word misspelled for which I do apologize. Nevertheless, my main concern is that it is not misspelled so badly that it fails to contribute constructively to the message it is intended to convey. Allow me to assume my readers will have enough grace to overlook my errors and enough intelligence to get over the rough spots and around the chuck holes and capture the essence of these writings. May God richly bless you as you graciously walk with me through my efforts to present God's truth and absolutes to you for counsel, guidance, and direction unto life and life more abundantly, giving glory, honor, and pleasure, to God, magnifying our Saviour Jesus, and edifying the body of Christ.

Although I am a fan of the Kings James Version, which I will use in the majority of my writing, I will not hesitate to refer to other Versions from time to time as occasionally I will find a word or phrase that seems more preferable to what needs to be said in order to get a better understanding of the message being given. An attempt will be made to identify the use of these various scriptures from the different versions with an explanation of why they are being used in preference to the

K.J.V. By doing this it is hoped we can "stay on the same page".

You will notice the use of much scripture throughout my writing with several scriptures being used many times in various situations. You may criticize this as redundancy if you wish. We were all born critics and man has developed it to a fine art, whether it be constructive or destructive, which it is in most cases as man has only to allow his nature to take its natural course to do this. However, what some may view as redundancy in the often use and application of Biblical truths, I simply see as **"emphasis"** to be diligently applied as needed substance for Christian character and development in all our lives. May God give you additional understanding of his word every time you come into contact with it. May it be often and consistent; for emphasis and effect, of course.

As a conclusion to this introduction, allow me once again to go to the scriptures, **[Hebrews 13: 20-21], "Now the God of peace, that brought again from the dead our Lord Jesus, that great shepherd of the sheep, through the everlasting covenant, Make you perfect in every good work to do his will, working in you that which is well pleasing in his sight, through Jesus Christ; to whom be glory for ever and ever. Amen.** I look forward to meeting you in heaven, and possibly before.

Sincerely, in God's love
Darold F. Edwards

NOTES

ii. ACKNOWLEDGMENTS

I would like to thank the people who from the very beginning as a novice writer were kind enough to read some of my earliest efforts and gave me some very encouraging reviews. First of course I would like to thank God for guiding me into writing. It has become a real Godsend to me and has provided direction and purpose for me at a time when otherwise, retirement could have been very trying. I need purpose in my life and writing of the nature you will see in these books gave me that. During my electrical career when I was able to help build some material churches, I thought that someday I would like to assist in building the spiritual church in the hearts and lives of people. God has opened the door to do that through writing for which I wish to express my soul depth gratitude.

Next, many heartfelt thanks to my dear wife Pat for encouraging me in everything along the way in our life together, what a strength and help she has been to me. Susan Canfield was one of the first, who has been very encouraging from the start. She also trims our Schnauzer, Max, which is another big help. This doesn't really have anything to do with my writing except it provides opportunity to visit with Susan from time to time to get additional input on the writing; she is always encouraging. Susan has been very helpful and encouraging in her comments and friendship. Thank you Susan.

Then there is Jock and Karen Elliot, some dear Christian friends who along with their family we have been blessed to know for many reasons including their encouragement in writing. Karen is also a great cook, which is another real advantage to knowing the right people, and I have been much blessed in this area by her talent. My son Myke is of an absolute necessity and blessing as he is my computer expert along with being my son and a very dear friend. I couldn't do this without him. Thanks Myke, for your ever patient and loving assistance along the way.

Then there is my dear friend and brother in the Lord, Clarence Parker, who comes over a couple of times a week just to talk, discuss, study Bible, and add his encouragement to me in my writing efforts. His comments are extremely uplifting and helpful. He also benefits from Karen's cooking, as do all who attend the Elliot's prayer meetings. What a great blessing and strength he is. Thank you my brother for standing alongside me during my writing struggles. Another dear friend, Nancy Gerling, has read some of my writings and has copies of my first efforts to have books published. She has always been extremely uplifting with her input concerning my writing. Many thanks to you, Nancy.

There are others that have added much to me with their encouraging comments about my works which are much appreciated. May God's blessings be upon them and may his presence fill their hearts and lives. May God's blessings also be added to you who are gracious enough to become a part of my reading public; let us study God's word together as he quickens us together in Christ, raises us up together, and makes us to sit together in heavenly places in Christ Jesus our Lord and Saviour, these places being made heavenly because of His presence, wherever that may be. May God's divine love abound in our hearts toward one another. Indeed; we do become a part of each other as we are a part of the body of Christ our Lord.

A little over a year ago as I was looking through a magazine advertising for a Restore America event, I run across another page where someone made the statement, **"How much information do we need before we get out of the boat and walk on the water"**. Whoever that person is, and wherever he may be, I would like to thank him for impacting my life with that inspirational word. Stepping out in faith and writing as I feel led of the Lord in my efforts is my way of walking on the water.

Your efforts are probably of a different calling than mine, but yet of the divine nature. May we blend our efforts and lives together in the unity Jesus prayed for in **John 17** for God's glory, honor, and pleasure. Come, walk with me as we journey along together with the multitudes who will join with us, as we all walk and sit together **"in heavenly places"**, inspiring each other as Jesus inspires us all. **To God be the glory forever and ever, Amen.**

NOTES

iii.   **PREFACE**

[Ecclesiastes 12: 11-12], "The words of the wise are as goads, and as nails fastened by the masters of the assemblies, which are given from one Shepard. And further, by these, my son, be admonished: of making many books there is no end; and much study is a weariness to the flesh". Much study demands considerable self discipline, diligence and determination, and a lot of invested time, whereas simply reading for the enjoyment of what is being read, or other lesser purposes, without the element of **"study to show thyself approved unto God", [2 Timothy 2: 15],** tends to a great waste of time.

However, such is not the case if a time of relaxation from business or other things that tend to stress is needed, and reading a good book that is a "no brainer" may be just the ticket. Unfortunately this becomes the norm for many people. As a result many books that neither contribute anything of value and add nothing constructive to the reader, are in great abundance and offer no challenge for growth and development. Consequently no study is required that would demand thought and concentration, so these books are read in pursuit of nothing, then put aside in favor of another "nothing" book or maybe just watching soap operas on T. V. or the equivalent in "nothing". Habits are thus formed with the result being wasted time and life.

Allow me to express extreme caution in the selection of your reading material as your reading is a direct input into the content of your mind and contributes heavily to "the abundance of your heart". So once again I say, proceed with wisdom, knowledge, understanding, and caution, applying some intelligence and plain common sense along the way, **[Proverbs**

4: 23], "Keeping thy heart with all diligence; for out of it are the issues of life". [Proverbs 2: 11], "Discretion shall preserve thee; understanding shall keep thee".

If we do not endeavor to establish our values and standards according to God's values and standards, we will exist in error continually without the life God has made available to us through Jesus Christ. It is with this in mind that I have set out to produce this work concerning the "RESURRECTION OF EXCELLENCY", to challenge the readers, whoever or wherever they may be: to look inside themselves and ask intelligent questions about their being, who they are, what they are, how they came to be, their purpose, and what their eternal destiny is, and what it is comprised of and by God's design. I find it very enlightening to realize I have by "intelligent design" been created as a very special and unique being instead as a blob of something left to chance as claimed by some who are also willing to risk their eternal destiny with their continuing low level of an unchallenged demented mentality.

Don't think me uncaring and insensitive to others because I use words such as stupidity, idiocy, and ignorant at times. We have all been there and if we are not careful and conscientious about our Christian training, have a tendency to revert back to old habits from time to time. I have nothing against man; only against the inadequate mentalities they have chosen to victimize themselves with. Even as Christians, former erroneous habits and desires, at times even with God's assistance, are hard to shake and it takes time, perseverance and diligence to cast them aside and grow out of them. They may or may not be classified as sin in all cases, but regardless consist of things that do not **"please the Lord," [John 8: 29], or "accompany salvation," [Hebrews 6: 9].** But in any event we need to **[2 Timothy 2: 15], "Study to show ourselves approved unto God, workmen that needeth not to be ashamed, rightly dividing the word of** truth." This involves the extensive effort of **[Romans 12: 2] "being transformed by the renewing of the mind", "exercising thyself unto Godliness", [1 Timothy 4: 7].**

The displacing of these life destroying discrepancies will only be accomplished with the diligent study and input of God's Word. These are just simply some destructive traits of humanity that if not addressed and dealt with according to God's counsel, will continue to plague their unsuspecting, unknowledgeable victims regardless of whether or not they are saved. The devil is not choosey who he victimizes and he will use any method at his disposal to re-devour anyone who becomes negligent in the **"keeping of the heart with all diligence", [Proverbs 4: 23].** Remember, as a Christian, you are his prime target, you are his priority. All others are already devoured. Such is the result of disregarding God's counsel and direction to **"choose life and blessing rather than death and cursing" [Deuteronomy 30: 19].**

I have had to reject the traditional terminology of "sinner saved by grace" in favor of **"a new creature in Christ, saved by Grace", [2 Corinthians 5: 17].** The reason for this was because the term "sinner" was not conducive to being **[1 John 1: 7-9], "forgiven of sin and cleansed from all unrighteousness by the blood of Jesus."** This is an insult to the power of the blood of Jesus to thoroughly cleanse from sin and unrighteousness in the name of Jesus for complete cleansing, forgiveness, deliverance and reconciliation. All this of course, is based on the condition of genuine, soul depth, repentance of sin and a commitment to **"fear [reverence] the Lord and work righteousness" [Acts 10: 35], serving the Lord with joyfulness and with gladness of heart, for the abundance of all things, [Deuteronomy 28: 47].** You may not agree with me on this issue and that's not important. Just be in agreement with God. It's his word that counts, not mine.

After all that God has done for us through Jesus Christ our Lord and Saviour in obtaining the **"divine nature of God through his great and precious promises"**, **[2 Peter 1:2 -4]**, it seemed that the title and name of "sinner" had some rather antagonistic and invasive qualities and connotations about it that never belonged nor fit in well with being **"a new creature in Christ saved by grace"**. The term "sinner" always suggested being stuck in a rut with no incentive to move on, whereas the new distinction and a new attitude concerning being "a new creature in Christ" provides a glorious challenge to, **[1Peter 1: 13], "Gird up the loins of our [spiritual] minds"** and, **[Hebrews 6: 1-3], "go on unto perfection"**, to the **[Job 4: 21], "Resurrection of the Excellency" which is in you, lest ye die, even without wisdom."**

NOTES

NOTES

I. GETTING A VISION OF THE VALUE

In the study of God's word with its essentials and absolutes, it is necessary to "Get a Vision of the Value" of this word of direction and correction for the time we have on this earth preparing us for our eternal future. The purpose of perceiving this value, all inclusive in **[Romans 2: 4], "the goodness of God that leadeth to repentance"** is to induce us to pursue the means to the end, or the goal, being the a life God desires and intends for us to enjoy versus a "survivalistic existence" of going through the motions, the programs and activities, without the peace and joy of being in intimacy of fellowship with God. This "value" is what God himself ascribes to his word and as such we need to examine this value without question and accept the value of it as God has determined it to be, for indeed this word is the Word of Life and life more abundantly.

In, **[Matthew 24:35]** we are given direct insight into the incomparable value that God gives to his word. **"Heaven and earth shall pass away, *but my words shall not pass away"*.** **[John 1:1-14]** gives us the direct connection and relationship in blending God and his word together. This will assist us in **"Getting a Vision of the Value" of this fullness of God, his divine nature, that we are to be partakers of, [Ephesians 3:19; 2Peter 1:4].** We dare not consider it of any less value than God himself determines it to be. It is the Word of truth and the Word of life. When every thing else is passed away, the winds of oppression and persecution are silenced and the dust of confusion and sin are settled in defeat, standing alone and victorious will be the Word of God, and if that Word is alive, well, and in operation within you, you also will be standing, more than a conqueror shouting the victory and giving God glory and honour as a king and priest unto him by Jesus Christ, **[Revelation 1: 6; 5: 9-10], "And hath made us kings and**

priests unto God and his Father; to him be glory and dominion for ever and ever, Amen.

God gives us some precise directions for living these words as our conduct, conversation, and lifestyle and the importance of them in **[Deuteronomy 30:19-20]**. The choosing of life and blessing is the choosing of loving his word with an enthusiastic attitude, **[Deuteronomy 28:47], "serving the Lord thy God with joyfulness and with gladness of heart for the abundance of all things" and the passing of the enthusiastic attitude of love and service on to your "seed"**. In verse **30:20** we find God's direction calling attention to an additional reason for the correct choice commanded in verse 19; **"That thou mayest love the Lord thy God, and that thou mayest obey his voice, [his WORD], and that thou mayest cleave unto him"**. In addition we see a threefold reason for all of this; **1, he is thy life, 2, he is the length of thy days, and 3, that we may live and move and have our being in Him, [Acts 17:28]**, dwelling in the area and place of service, with the calling where God has placed our individual lives for our own good and his divine purpose and pleasure, **[1 Corinthians 12]**. Obedience to his directions and counsel, Word, results in **"fearing [revering] Him",[John: 8:29], "doing always those things that please him"**, and the **"working of righteousness", [Acts 10:35], "thus being accepted with Him"**.

We should see great value in this as Jesus, providing our perfect example said, **"He that sent me is always with me, the Father hath not left me alone for [because] I do always those things that please him"**. It would seem that upon close examination of this scripture we see it as the way to always enjoy the presence of the Father, simply learning and DOING always those things that please him. We spend years of time, energy, and fortunes to learn things that are not nearly as advantageous as gaining this knowledge of God. Many of these things may well be helpful in everyday living, but so many of them, being misused or abused, are downright destructive to ourselves and others under our influence. This cultivating of God's favor and presence will be the most intelligent decision and choice you will ever make; this availing yourself of God's provision for your personal salvation through Jesus Christ for the forgiveness of sin, repentance and **[Deuteronomy 28:47]** "*always* **serving the Lord thy God with joyfulness, and gladness of heart for the abundance of all things"**. We can get a glimpse of what the glories of heaven are going to be like but we won't know the entirety of it until we get there. However, there is enough of it revealed by the Spirit of God, **[1 Corinthians 2:10]** by his various methods to create quite a desire to be there. We can also get a look at the horrors of hell, but those who go there can't be aware of the full magnitude of the experience until they are trapped for eternity in the midst of its unimaginable sufferings, horrors, and misery. If a person would meditate on this for awhile, it might assist them in **"getting a vision of the value"** of God's word of deliverance.

The world places no value on this Word of God, the Bible, but rather despises it, and rejecting it, and even in some professing Christians, just neglecting it to the point they suffer the same problems that they would if they had rejected it in the beginning, **[1 Peter 4:17-19].** To get this "vision of value" we must exercise our mentalities to learn to see things the way God sees them, thinking about them as He does and conducting our ways accordingly, allowing God to assign the "values" and then subscribing to those values for enrichment and a God pleasing quality of life. We find in **[1 Corinthians 3:10-15] "Jesus being described as the foundation upon which we are to build our lives, vs. 10, But let every man take heed how he buildeth there-upon".** Verse 12 compares the "good works" of the Christian life, **[Ephesians 2:10]** to gold, silver, and precious stones or to wood, hay, and stubble. **Verses 13-14** speaks of what sort of works these are, whether or not they will stand the tests they will be put to, if they will survive or be burnt up. The works of value, gold, silver and precious stones that survive will bring rewards, whereas the valueless, non-productive works of wood, hay, and stubble will be burnt up and bear no rewards but the person themselves shall be saved; yet so as by fire.

There is an interesting concept here to be explored as to the difference between Christians who are, new creations saved by grace whose works of gold, silver, and precious stones merit rewards versus those whose works are of wood, hay, and stubble that are burnt up without rewards, but they themselves shall be saved "so as by fire". These may well be the "sinners saved by grace" as all Christians are traditionally referred to as being, howbeit without God's grace no man could be saved. Nevertheless, it is imperative that we **"be about the Fathers business, [Luke 2:9], adorning the doctrine of God our Saviour in all things, [Titus 2:10], with the good works that God has before ordained that we should walk in"**, **[Ephesians 2: 10]**.

Some questions arise here that are very interesting as to a person's idea of who and what they are, or what they consider themselves to be, based on all the former years of traditional input and conditioning. It must be understood that these works are not performed in an attempt to be saved but can only be performed as a result of being saved. Too many people get hung up on grace versus works and go to great lengths to get their point of view across to others. Such arguments usually do nothing but cause strife and confusion which has no place in the family of God. Express your view if there is a need, there rarely is, and drop it, the Holy Spirit can convey truth much better than we can, **[John 16:13; 14: 26]**. It is just that these works are to be a labor of love as an expression of gratitude to God for his gift of amazing grace, but never as an attempt to earn it.

These works qualify as **"doing always those things that please him", and [Hebrews 6:9]"things that accompany salvation", as [Matt. 7:17] "good fruit bearing trees"**, all for, and always for the purpose of bringing glory, honour, and pleasure to God. **[Ephesians 2:8-10], "For by grace are ye saved through faith; and that not of yourselves: it is the gift of God: not of works, lest any man should boast. For we are his workmanship created in Christ Jesus unto good works, which God hath before ordained that we should walk in them", [1Timothy 4:7] exercising thyself unto Godliness, [1 Timothy 4:7] or "God-like-ness".** Study the book of James for some additional interesting counsel on the subject of these "good works" and the need for them.

Generally speaking, people will attach value to that for which they have an affinity or desire, even if that which is desired is destructive. This is consistent with our "if it feels good do it" culture and society America has degraded into. Consequently drug pushers and addicts will attach great value to the drugs that are destroying them, and others likewise will devise various harmful and destructive lifestyles for profit and pleasure regardless of who it destroys, including themselves. These people will place great value on such a lifestyle as it caters to the satisfaction of the desires of the flesh. Once again, the blind leading the blind principle comes into focus. The condition and abundance of the heart, the mind, however, must be considered here as to sound reasoning and intelligent choice.

Where value is perceived, even by the deluded mind in a destructive direction, pursuit in that direction is normal using all the means available, honest or dishonest, to attain to the end pursued. Where value is not perceived, intense pursuit is unlikely, even if it is of such worldly pursuits as fun, games excitement, intrigue, and other forms of entertainment, some of which is, under certain circumstances, acceptable.

There is, however, by the serious Bible directed mind, great value seen in the pursuit of that which affords **great and perfect peace, [Psalms 119:165; Isaiah 26:3], and fullness of joy, [Psalms 16:11],** which adds strength and encouragement to the spirit, and direction, purpose, and profit to the soul. The greater value, delight, and esteem given to God's Word the more likely time and effort are to be expended in that direction for meditation, and study to attain to that for which it was intended, **[Matthew 6: 33], "seeking first the kingdom of God and his righteousness" for the wisdom, understanding, and knowledge that is necessary to prevent destruction, [Hosea 4:6].**

Attention and pursuit executed is dependent on, and commensurate with, the perceived value given. If value on **"things above"** is not sufficiently perceived through the eyes of understanding, **[Ephesians 1:18],** attention and affection will be focused elsewhere and efforts, energies, and fortunes will be directed toward that where value is seen, such as things on the earth, be they good or evil, **[Colossians 3:2]. The renewing of the mind, [Romans 12:2]** is of immense value in itself for without this we cannot comprehend the things of God unto salvation, nor can we establish value where value is essential.

On the other hand, there are other people who never expose themselves to mind altering devices that adversely affect a thought process who will consistently reject God and his provision of redemption and reconciliation, choosing **[Deuteronomy 30:19]** death and cursing rather than life and blessing. The neglect of choosing life and blessing so that both they and their children shall live results in the remaining in the condition of the alternative of death and cursing which will also be passed on to your "seed". We can see from this that some, not all, people who appear to be intelligent can show an extreme lack of actual intelligence when it comes to diligently seeking God and his blessings and provisions.

Some may take exception to the insinuation that to exist in rejection of Jesus Christ and salvation of the soul with the life and life more abundantly it provides shows an extreme lack of intelligence even unto stupidity. But when you consider the eternal destructive nature of the action, or lack of it, and that it affects also the lives of the children involved unto death and destruction, it's pretty hard to dispute it. We see multitudes of young people today that are trapped in the linage of such foolishness and digression initiated by parents, and possibly grandparents or great grandparents before them, not making the right choice for "life and blessing", **[Exodus 20: 5; 34:7], [Numbers 14: 18], [Deuteronomy 5: 9], [Hosea 4: 6].** This was all to common among the Old Testament kings, the vast majority of which were a wretched rebellious lot that led all their people into sin and idolatry, for which the whole nation paid dearly. Much is to be considered here for contemplation and fits in exceedingly well with **[2 Timothy 3: 16], "All scripture is given by inspiration of God, and is profitable for doctrine, for reproof, for correction, for instruction in righteousness: That the man of God may be perfect, thoroughly furnished unto all good works".** Therefore, **[2 Timothy 2: 15], "Study to show thyself approved unto God, a workman that needeth not to be ashamed, rightly dividing the word of truth".**

There is considerable value in considering, that although you don't particularly believe in God; that all this talk about salvation, heaven, hell, etc, just might be true; it might just be a wise thing to take appropriate action to investigate it for the protection of yourself and your family. There is a certain amount of value and intelligence exercised in just considering it. After all, you've got nothing to lose and everything to gain. It doesn't take much intelligence to see the value of choosing life and blessing instead of remaining in the condition of death and cursing you were born with. Whether or not heaven and hell are realities or exist only as possibilities, intelligent choice would opt in favor of the better of the two "possibilities" just in case they both turned out to be realities. You certainly don't want to be caught with your mentality locked into the wrong choice because of some stupid pride that prevents you from making a course correction in life's journey that effects your eternity as well as the eternity of your family. Now ask yourself, what would the intelligent choice be; and if you don't make the appropriate choice when you are well able to, in a sense, sawing the limb off behind you, would you be wise, or otherwise?

NOTES

NOTES

II. THE STANDARD

[Isaiah 59: 19], "--When the enemy shall come in like a flood, the Spirit of the Lord shall lift up a standard against him." Certainly the first part of this verse and the preceding verses back to verse 19 refer to Christ as the "standard" referred to here as well as the two following verses, 20 and 21. It seems that there has always been a "remnant" of people among the multitudes and masses of humanity that have rose to the occasion to stand with God in righteousness along side Jesus in contributing to and supportive of that "STANDARD". We find Jesus referring to this in a specific manner in **[Matthew 16:18], "Upon this rock [the truth of God concerning who Jesus is], I will build MY CHURCH, and the gates of hell [all weapons of opposition], shall not prevail against it". [Isaiah 54: 15-17], but "whosoever shall gather together against thee shall fall for thy sake", No weapon that is formed against thee shall prosper; and every tongue that shall rise against thee in judgment THOU SHALT CONDEMN.** *This is the heritage of the servants of the Lord, and their righteousness is of me, saith the Lord.*

There is no doubt in my mind about this **[Matthew 16: 18]** church being alive and well today throughout the world. I do wonder about the extent of its existence in our "land of the free and the home of the brave", however. When the clay has, by a perverted constitutional amendment, cast the potter out of the house and decided it will mold itself into whatever its self imposed relativity allows it to be according to its own will, it cannot by any stretch of the imagination, be a part of that church. They may don their regalia and go through all the outward motions while putting on a great show of piety and pomp, and assume their positions of superior wisdom and knowledge, but if this is all a production of a deceitful heart, they have only dug their pit deeper and lured others in with them.

It all depends on the abundance of the heart, **[Luke 6: 45]**, **"A good man out of the good treasure of his heart bringeth forth that which is good; and an evil man out of the evil treasure of his heart bringeth forth that which is evil: for of the abundance of the heart the mouth speaketh"**; [his mind thinks, his mouth speaks, and his hand does]. A person will live, or struggle, through their life according to their line of thinking, whether good or evil, right or wrong. The **"things that pertain unto life and godliness" in [2 Peter 1: 3],** including our "remembrance", reliance, and confidence in **the exceeding great and precious promises of verse 4 whereby we might be partakers of God's own divine nature,** are the things that the thief, **[John 10: 10], "comes for to steal, kill, and destroy."** Once he has done this, you are also destroyed, for in essence, you are the abundance and substance of the content of your heart and mind, **[Proverbs 23: 7], "For as a man thinketh in his heart, so is he"**. [Matthew 15: 8-9]!

It is a sad thing when we witness our "accomplished" theologians in disagreement over non-essentials, and using that as an occasion to snipe at each other and thus chip away at the unity Jesus is praying for in **[John 17]** that is so essential to the success of the church. This "sniping", or "verbal mudslinging", **[Galatians 5: 15], "bite and devour" with words,** smacks of corrupt political activity in the world and has no place in the redeemed community of Christ but only forms additional "gates of hell" and "strongholds" that need to be torn down. There may well be a difference of opinion in some areas, but the greatest error is to have a breakdown of unity over non-essentials by taking spiritual pot-shots at each other without allowing each other difference of opinions on points that have nothing to do with salvation.

There are certain essentials that must be dealt with that will demand a separation among groups. There must for the sake of that which God requires for relationship with him, be a separation from that which he himself despises. There are reasons why we are told in **[1 Peter 4:17], "For the time is come that judgment must begin at the house of God: and if it first begin at us, what shall the end be of those that obey not the gospel of God? And if the righteous scarcely be saved, where will the ungodly and the sinner appear?"**

It is important for all of us to realize that it is not the amount of knowledge we have or think we have about prophecy, eschatology, apologetics, etc, etc, and a multitude of additional things man has to debate and have dialogue about and impress each other with that really matters. These things are interesting and important to a point. Beyond that they can become detrimental to victorious life. What is important is that we **[2 Timothy 2: 15], "Study to show "ourselves" thyself approved unto God, a workman that needeth not to be ashamed, rightly dividing the word of truth",** but be committed to the establishment of **John 17 unity** within the family of the redeemed.

A good place to start would be to make a study of **"the *things* that accompany salvation" [Hebrews 6: 9]** and **"the *things* that always please God, [John 8: 29].** A conscientious study of these "things", not to impress others with our vast knowledge of them, but for the purpose of incorporating and blending our lives, thoughts, conversation, an conduct together with them in the manifesting of God's divine nature, **[2 Peter 1: 2-11],** within us as individuals, and as the unified **[Matthew 16: 18] "Church of Jesus Christ"**. This should keep us busy for a lifetime of **[Jude 1: 20], "building up ourselves in the most holy faith, praying in the Holy Ghost" and "exhorting**

one another" that we might live lives that are contributive of that which pleases God and encourages each other.

It is tragic that the first sixteen verses of **[Isaiah 59]** are a very accurate description of America today. There are many others portions of scripture contained within God's word that give vivid, frightening accounts of the present state and condition of our America. Several years ago I remember there arose a controversy about the proper location of the comma in the above chapter, **verse, 19,** whether it should be between the word "in and like", or remain as is presently and customarily shown in the King James version of the bible. Personally I couldn't care less. At the time of the controversy it looked like a waste of time and energy, distracting from the essentials of Christian growth and development, and proving nothing and doing nothing but providing more controversy and contention like the controversy over at what point of time in reference to the great tribulation, the rapture will take place, whether pre-, mid, or post. Who cares, that is God's agenda; ours is to be ready when it does happen.

Whatever or whoever the standard was to be or intended to be, it was without a doubt, greater and mightier than whatever the enemy could muster up, regardless whether it was a flood or not, or what this flood is to consist of. We would have been much better off to have addressed the question of "what is, was, or, who is, this "standard", and concentrate our attention and energies on being that standard, if we are indeed a part of the standard being referred to, or at least assisting and giving support to that standard instead of trying to prove a useless point of where this comma belonged. Certainly we have more important issues to address. Don't allow yourself to be sidetracked with nonsense that. **"adds nothing to you" [Galatians 2: 6].**

It would seem that Jesus addressed this subject in **[Matthew 16:18]** when he stated that he was going to build **HIS CHURCH, "HIS STANDARD",** upon the rock of truth that he was indeed "**the Christ, the Son of the living God**" as revealed by the Father himself, and the gates of hell, the enemy, whether in the form of a flood or not, "**shall not prevail against IT."** It would seem that Jesus is referring to a very special group or **"church" that are "more than conquerors through him that loved us", that busy themselves by studying and gaining proficiency in the use of "the whole armor of God [Ephesians 6:13-17].** Unfortunately, our sword, our weapon of offense, this **handbook of spiritual warfare**, has become dull and nearly useless in our hands because of our reluctance to use it for fear we might be "offensive" to the world around us.

The truth has always been, is today, and will always be, offensive to those who oppose it, for it awakens the truth of their transgressions and iniquity within them and exposes it in a manner they can neither avoid nor escape, but nevertheless, the conviction of their error makes them very uncomfortable because they cannot hide from it. **"Truth, crushed to earth will rise again. The eternal years of God are hers, while error, wounded, writhes in pain and dies among his worshippers".** They may not, because of their arrogance and pride, admit to it but they cannot help but feel its convicting power. In Biblical reference, we speak of this as Holy Spirit conviction of sin, and it is a very uncomfortable position to be in, so in their attempt to escape from the truth of their abominations, they wage war against this truth in an attempt to silence it, or at least suppress it.

The problem is that the longer the Christians remain withdrawn from the battle lines in silence, the more our proficiency wanes in the use of the weapons of our warfare, **thus giving Satan advantage of us, [2 Corinthians 2: 11].** If people are offended by the truth of God's word of absolutes, that is their problem, but the truth should never be withheld or suppressed because it offends those who need it most; the unsaved for salvation and the saved for additional spiritual development, growth, commitment, and progress unto spiritual maturity. It may be that there are times that it must be presented with discretion, but never withheld. Truth has always been and always will be offensive to that which is opposed to it.

If we are afraid or ashamed to present the truth as God intended we should, rest assured, the gates of hell shall prevail. We need to study **Jeremiah's** commission **[Jeremiah 1]** to get a flavor of what is required in the face of opposition and God's attitude about those who are "offended" by the truth of the gospel, or hesitant to declare and proclaim it. Maybe this is the difference between a house or church built by man and a house or church built by God, **[Psalms 127:1]**. There is no doubt about it, if the house, the church, is not built by the Lord on the Rock of his eternal truth, it is built by man on the sand of deception, subject to his extremely inferior specifications, and can never be the standard that is to be raised by the Holy Spirit. It will sooner or later fall because of the winds, rain, and storms of deception, opposition, and falsehood imposed by mans will, pride and fear of "offending" someone. The church has come under the attack of "political correctness", an insidious, evil invention to suppress God's truth and absolutes and herd the redeemed community of Christ into "the corral of compliance".

Many are the churches that have had to weather the interior storms of error that have been imposed by their "own countrymen". It is bad enough when the world attacks, but when there is no unity among the brethren unto peace and harmony and they attack each other; this is abomination indeed, and fits exactly the description of a prevailing gate of hell. What could be more displeasing to God and pleasing to "the thief" than to sneak into a church and steal the peace, kill the unity and harmony, and destroy the love for one another? What terrible struggles go on at the present time in individuals, marriages, families, homes, churches and indeed our nation because man will not reach down into his heart, confess his sin and iniquity and repent with the whole heart and believe in the gospel of Jesus unto willing obedience, **and gladly receiving the Word, [Acts 2:41]. [Hosea 4: 6-7], "My people are destroyed for lack of knowledge: because thou hast rejected knowledge, I will also reject thee, that thou shalt be no priest to me: seeing thou hast forgotten the law "Word" of thy God, I will also forget thy children. As they were increased, so they sinned against me: therefore will I change their glory into shame".** This includes our government and all departments within it as well as our judicial and educational structures.

It is amazing that this man that God originally created as an intelligent being has become so deranged and disgusting so as to sacrifice his future both now and eternally just to keep and exercise his selfishness and pride for a few short miserable years on this earth, and contributing to the destruction of all those within his influence, **beginning with the children, Hosea 4:6].** I am often reminded of a quotation from Shakespeare, **"What fools ye mortals be"**. It makes me wonder about his knowledge of God's word, **[Proverbs 1:7 "The fear of the Lord is the beginning of knowledge: but fools despise wisdom and instruction."** It certainly gives credibility to this Shakespearean quotation. Man has historically up to, and for certain in our present day, demonstrated his overwhelming capacity and lust, for foolishness, stupidity, and idiocy. **[Hosea 4:7] "As they increased so they sinned against me: therefore I will change their glory into shame."**

With all God's warnings to the unrighteous and his provision for their redemption and reconciliation, and his promises that cannot fail to the repentant righteous, indeed, "what fools ye mortals be". It is testimony to the thief's proficiency in stealing, killing, and destroying with, of course, the willing assistance of "his children" who are of their father, the devil, **[John 8: 44]**. Would to God, that the Christians would become as proficient in "being about their Father's business" in diligence, dedication, and willing obedience as the sinners are in serving their father, the devil. Is there possibly an additional "standard" that is spoken of and implied in **[Isaiah 59:19]**? In **[Matthew 5:13-14],** Christians are spoken of as the "salt of the earth", and" the light of the world". Surely within the context of these two descriptions we should be able to find something that would qualify as pertaining to the "standard" referred to in **[Isaiah 59:19]**.

If those **[John 8:41-47],** note vs. 44, who are of their father, the devil, are willing to sacrifice their entire time on this earth and suffer the horrors of eternity as well to serve him; *we Christians should, in light of the great and precious promises of God that are ours exclusively, be prompted to study to be willingly obedient to our Father which is in heaven.*

This should by all means be our absolute priority in life. Without this as our priority, we have no life, but become as those that oppose the essentials of Christian life and living. **[Romans 6:16-23], esp. vs.19, " I speak after the manner of men because of the infirmity of your flesh: for as ye yielded your members servants to uncleanness and to iniquity unto iniquity; even so now yield your members servants to righteousness unto holiness"**. It would seem as though we are to serve God with at least the same commitment, dedication, and effort with which we in the past, served the devil. This should be the minimum required even of ourselves. This is well within the realm of possibility as: **[2 Peter 1:3] "According as his, God's, divine power hath given unto us all things that** pertain unto life and godliness, through the knowledge of him that hath called us to glory and virtue".

Herein lay the problems that plague both the world and the Christian family: **"not enough of the knowledge of him that hath called us to glory and virtue"**. It would seem as though we have failed to **"set our affection on the things above"** but have in our business and neglect**, set our affection on the things of the earth", [Colossians 3:2] "where moth and rust doth corrupt**, [and depreciation] **and thieves break through and steal".**

It might well be appropriate here to ask the question; what would constitute a standard in this situation? In **[Nahum 1:7-8],** we find in verse 8 that the Lord used an "overrunning flood" as a standard to correct a situation created by an enemy that came in like a flood. The account of this is found in **[Isaiah 37:36],** the flood being Sennacherib, king of Assyria with his army, and the "overrunning flood", **one angel of the Lord who turned back the flood by slaying, during the night, one hundred eighty five thousand** of Sennachrib's army, and they didn't even know it happened until the remainder awoke the next morning. And we are afraid to even offend someone. Being an enemy in opposition against God and his righteousness is not an intelligent place to be. **[James 4:7]:** *Submitting yourselves to God is a prerequisite to the beginning of the raising up of a standard against the enemy and causing him to flee, and begins with a soul depth repentance of sin and accepting Jesus as Saviour and King.*

Jesus made this prerequisite quite clear in **[Mark 1:15] when he said"------repent ye and believe the gospel"**. God made it quite plain in **[Deuteronomy 30:19]** when he counseled mankind to **choose life and blessing instead of death and cursing;** the correct choice itself being a "raising of a standard" against the enemy, for the choice alone implies a submission to God and obedience immediately following repentance, **[Acts 2:41[, "Then they that gladly received his word were baptized: and the same day there were added unto them about three thousand souls"**. For the four ingredients of repentance see **[2 Chronicles 7: 14], "If my people, which are called by my name, #1-*shall humble themselves, #2-and pray, #3-and seek my face, #4-and turn from their wicked ways*; THEN will I hear from heaven, and will forgive their sin, and will heal their land"**. There are conditions to being forgiven of sin and having our nation healed of her iniquities and the results of them.

In many scriptures throughout the Bible it speaks of worshiping, praising, serving, etc, the Lord with the whole heart. This constitutes living a life, a standard, against the enemy, diligently and continually. **[Acts 17:28] "For in him we live, and move, and have our being"**. In him we live and move and maintain a Biblical standard of attitude, conversation, and conduct against the enemy and adversary of our souls; that wicked one who steals, kills, and destroys. He is the accuser of the brethren. In view of the deceitfulness of "Satan", **[2 Corinthians 11:13-15], "Who himself is transformed into an angel of light", [1Peter 5: 8], "Be sober, be vigilant, because your adversary the devil, as a roaring lion, walketh about seeking whom he may devour."** If you are a Christian, you are his target, for all others are already devoured, lost in the absolute senselessness of sin and the iniquity that is also found in their father the devil, **[Ezekiel 28:15], [John 8:44]. [Ephesians 2:1-7], Vs.1-3 "And you hath he quickened , who were dead in trespass and sins; Wherein in times past, ye also walked according to the course of this world, according to the prince of the power of the air, this enemy, Satan, the spirit that now worketh in the children of disobedience". Among whom also we all had our conversation in time past** in the lust of our flesh, fulfilling the desires of the flesh and of the mind; and were by nature the children of wrath, even as others". 4-7, "**BUT GOD**, who is rich in mercy, for his great love wherein he loved us, even when we were dead in sins, hath quickened us together with Christ, [by grace are ye saved]. And hath raised us up together, and made us to sit together in heavenly places in Christ Jesus: That in ages to come he might show the exceeding riches of his grace in his kindness toward us in Christ Jesus".

Some may think it rather insensitive of me in my summation of mankind to use such words as stupid, idiocy, ignorant, etc; however, I've been around for quite awhile and my observation plus my years of experience has shown me that humanity has a tremendous propensity for manifesting these plus a few other very adverse, descriptive, characteristics. There are, of course, exceptions to this and the possibility of choosing, learning and growing out of the general category into the exceptional category is a readily available and a desirable and distinct possibility for those who choose to do so. Now we have a general category and an exceptional category. Let's see where the difference lies. There is a choice that forms the dividing line between the two and we find that dividing line between verses 3 and 4 of the afore mentioned scriptures of **[Ephesians 2:1-7]**.

To get a better look at, and understanding of the seriousness of being on the correct side of that division, let's start by going to **[Deuteronomy 30:19-20]**. God here, out of his intense love and concern for his creation is giving us an everlasting, beneficial, principle that is based on the intelligence, or desperation, of being obedient to his counsel which is basically where a person passes from the general to the exceptional category alluded to early. **"I call heaven and earth to record this day against you, that I have set before you life and death, blessing and cursing: THEREFORE CHOOSE LIFE,**

that both thou [you] and thy [your] seed [children, descendents] may live.

Throughout my writings I will consistently use some scriptures that need to be **"EMPHASIZED"** during teaching and learning about life. Maybe this would be better understood if we talked of these scriptures as being "where the rubber meets the road" of life. It is interesting that this "choice" may be based on intelligent thinking concerning a desire to live above and beyond the conditions of this sin ridden world that is destroying people and souls by the millions or a flash of intelligence expressed in a desperate choice to escape this worldly existence wherein we were born and trapped.

Either way, God through his providence provided the opportunity and inducement to make that choice which you will find out more about as you learn and grow in his school room of life and life more abundantly. You don't have to know nor understand anything at this point, only respond to the prompting to do what Jesus tells us all in **[Mark 1:15], "Repent and believe the gospel".** In Shakespeare's manner of speaking, as in "to be or not to be", that is the question; here we have "to repent or not to repent", that is indeed the question. This is the door we pass through as we advance from the "general category" of death and cursing, **[Eph. 2:1-3],** to the "exceptional category" of life and blessings, **verses 4-10].**

Now that we have passed through the doorway of sincere repentance from sin, death and cursing, if indeed you have, and entered into the classroom of believing the gospel of obedience unto life and blessing, it is time to rejoice. Take a seat and open up God's textbook, the Holy Bible as the Holy Spirit, the master teacher of the universe with all wisdom, knowledge, understanding, intelligence, and yes, common sense, proceeds to give us our daily assignments, including new revelations that become such an important part of our new educational series as we learn to **"set your affections on things above and not on things on the earth", [Colossians 3: 2].** May God bless you richly as you become an "exception" in life, believing, learning and living his gospel of truth and absolutes of righteousness and holiness unto the glory, honour, and pleasure of God "for thy good". I do not apologize for the use of the terms mentioned earlier as to man's characteristics concerning those things that pertain to God, I have been there.

If confession is good for the soul, so be it, but I have experienced my times of stupidity, idiocy, ignorance, and maybe a few others including extended periods of just plain dumb. Such is the extent of my confession without any details included. You, because you are human, undoubtedly will have enough of your own to contend with without being overly concerned about mine, some of which will be similar to mine. Even though we have passed from death and cursing unto life and blessing, these symptoms and characteristics still have a tendency to hand around and ambush us at the most inopportune times, possibly resulting in considerable embarrassment and maybe a little remorse added for effect. However, in spite of all this, because of God's grace and provision, **[1John 2:1-2], "My little children, these write I unto you, that ye sin not, And if any man sin, we have an advocate with the Father, Jesus Christ the righteousness: And he is the propitiation for our sins: and not for ours only, but also for the sins of the whole world"**.

But such is life and if we are still alive and functioning somewhat normal we can expect one or more of these human traits to manifest themselves again from time to time. They may not constitute sin, but it would still be nice to be rid of them, some of which will be accomplished in God's school room; maybe depending on how hard and diligent you study, however many of these things will be eliminated only by what is gained through God's counsel and training in obedience to his word. I have heard people mention "the school of hard knocks"; though we will all experience some of this, many of these hard knocks will be alleviated by the upgrading of our conduct as a Biblical, Godly, pattern of thinking and thoughts is learned, and thus new ways are established as a new lifestyle is formed.

It is a total change in favor of new cause and effects, a **[Romans 12:2]** renewing the mind unto Biblical principles, truths, and absolutes. **[2 Timothy 2:15]: Biblical input with new thinking and thoughts [cause] new personalities and ways [effects], [Isaiah 55:7-8]. As new creatures in Christ, [2 Corinthians 5:17-18]** as the old things, thinking, thoughts, and ways of sin are repented of and washed away by the blood of Jesus, the new thinking, thoughts, and ways we receive are from the heart of God and become new causes producing new effects of working righteousness, **[Acts 10: 34-35] which are acceptable unto God**, and displacing the old mannerisms of sin and iniquity which were characteristic of our "before repentance" existence**, [Ephesians 2:1-3].**

This brings about a whole new dimension of life and living with the "school of hard knocks" of the world being displaced and greatly replaced by the elements of Godliness, wisdom, knowledge, understanding, and intelligence. With these things taking place in our mentalities, we are now able to learn from the bumps on the other fellows head instead of taking our own "hard knocks" with lumps on our own heads.

Even in the family of God we have our "general category" that doesn't do well in school, still taking lumps on their own heads, and our "exceptional category" that studies hard to learn and execute the things learned to produce the good works of silver, gold, and precious stones we were created unto that God before ordained that we should walk in, **[1 Corinthians 3:12-13; Ephesians 2:10].** We find individuals of all categories throughout the Bible and our nation and world today. It doesn't seem as though humanity has learned anything from the worldly school of hard knocks; they still turn their backs on God and despise his word and America is no exception.

[Hosea 4:6-10]. As we have increased, so has our sin and rebellion against God increased in intensity, and we can see the glory of our great nation dwindling as a result and being turned into shame. Once again we can see cause and effect in action; but we can't seem, as a nation, to muster up the intelligence and zeal to correct its downward spiral. Neither the "leaders" nor the general populace in excluding God and his counsel, have what it takes to reverse the dilemmas we face. Only God is the answer and as long as man continues in his excommunication and rejection of God and his righteous counsel because of stupidity, ignorance, and idiocy, we will have no answer, and certainly no solutions, **[Job 5:6-7; Isaiah 50: 11].**

NOTES

III. ESSENTIALS

[Proverbs 4:7], **"Wisdom is the principal thing; therefore get wisdom: and with all thy getting get understanding".** Wisdom and understanding are two of the many essentials that are needed in order to develop a successful Christian life. Others will include, discretion, knowledge, intelligence, and the furnishings of the **[Matthew 7:24]** house built upon a [the] Rock. These furnishings begin with the **[Galatians 5: 22-23], "fruit of the Spirit, love, joy, peace, longsuffering, gentleness goodness, faith, meekness, and temperance: against such there is no law".** There are others that are not included here such as patience, forgiveness, kindness; and the list goes on and on. These could all be considered as "fruit of the Spirit" along with others to be found throughout God's word but not included here. All of these "things" are included in the **"things that accompany salvation and the things that always please God", [Hebrews 6: 9; John 8: 29].** There are many other things that will be discovered through intense study and revealed by the Holy Spirit through much meditation.

Diligence in study is a part of this in order to search out these nuggets of truth, blending them into your being for the purpose of having life and life more abundantly and partaking of the divine nature of God. Jesus set the stage for this through his own sacrifice for all the sins of all mankind forever, telling us how to avail ourselves of that which he made available to us on the cross. In **[John 4: 32; 34]** Jesus gives some very enlightening information concerning his, and subsequently our, relationship with the Father. When offered food by his disciples "he said unto them, I have meat to eat that ye know not of". Then in response to their questions to each other about this, he continued: **"Jesus saith unto them, My meat is to do the will of him that sent me, and to finish his work".** This meat of which he spoke in doing the will of his Father who sent him was the "doing always the things that pleased the Father", being willingly obedient to God's desires and wishes. This guaranteed him the presence of the Father that strengthened and sustained him; in short, the total spiritual sustenance he needed and required to fulfill his mission, finishing the work God sent him to do.

He was not discounting the need for physical needs and nourishment here, but was simply showing the importance of spiritual pursuits and accomplishment in comparison to the physical things we have been conditioned to believe are so important. **[Mark 1:15], "Repent ye and _believe_ the gospel".** This word "believe" as used here requires considerable consideration and in-depth study as to its implications and demands. I am sure we all believed our parents existed, but that does not mean we were always obedient to them and their wishes. There is no doubt that to "believe" in the context it is presented here has direct correlation to being gladly receptive to his word with an attitude of willing obedience, **[Deuteronomy 28:47], "serving the Lord our God with joyfulness and gladness of heart for the abundance of all things".** It certainly goes well beyond the idea of just acknowledging the existence of something.

So you claim to believe in God, big deal! **[James 2:19], "Thou believest that there is one God; thou doest well: the devils also believe and tremble".** They believe in him to an extent that we can't imagine; they have been getting their "heads bruised": the world has different terminology for this, every since their boss, Lucifer, better known as Satan or the devil conned them into joining his lost cause and people have been signing on with him every since, _in the same lost cause._ The profound stupidity of what was initially created to be an intelligent creature never ceases to amaze me.

It is all testimony of the ability of the master deceiver, this same Lucifer, in his ability to blind and deceive. We've all been there, done that, and still revert back to it occasionally and unfortunately, with some never leaving it. **[Ephesians 2:1-3], "And you hath he quickened, who were dead in trespass and sins; Wherein times past ye walked according to the course of this world, according to the prince of the power of the air, the spirit that now worketh in the children of disobedience: Among whom we all had our conversation in times past in the lusts of the flesh, fulfilling the desires of the flesh and the mind; and were by nature the children of wrath even as others.**

Verse 4 continues with these all important words, "BUT GOD, BUT GOD", this great majestic, ever intervening GOD, who by his providence, interrupts our sinful lifestyles and redirects our paths unto righteousness, holiness, and life eternal, unto him be GLORY, and POWER, and HONOUR, AND DOMINION forever, beginning in our own individual hearts and minds, and thus, our lives, societies, cultures, and nations.

This item of "wisdom" must be the first to be considered, for the requirement for attaining to it or the acquiring of it is the basis of our entire being. **[Psalms 111:10], The fear of the Lord is the beginning of wisdom: a good understanding have all they that do his commandments: his praise endureth forever."** I would prefer to use the word "reverence" in the place of "fear" in the above scripture. It seems to be more fitting considering the present day general understanding of the word "fear". We might get a better understanding of this if we were to bring in **[Matthew 22:37]; "Jesus said unto him, Thou shalt love the Lord thy God with all thy heart, and with all thy soul, and with all thy mind".**

It is to a certain extent hard to imagine the relationship commanded here to take place based on "fear', however, it is well within the idea of "loving God" that this whole concept of revering him and returning this love to him in intimacy of relationship can be understood. By all means wisdom is the principal thing, and the revering of God is just the beginning of this wisdom. **[Proverbs 4: 7], "Wisdom is the principle thing; therefore get wisdom: and with all thy getting get understanding"**. The continuation of this wisdom, knowledge, and understanding is based on **[Psalms 1:2; 119:165] "delighting and meditating in, loving God's Word and being diligent in", [2 Timothy 2: 15], "studying to shew thyself approved unto God, a workman that needeth not to be ashamed, rightly dividing the word of truth"**.

[Matthew 22: 37-40] gives us additional counsel and direction for its continued enrichment and development as we learn to love God and move closer to him, **"Jesus said unto him, Thou shalt love the Lord thy God with all thy heart, with all thy soul and all thy mind. This is the first and great commandment. The second is like unto it, Thou shalt love thy neighbor as thyself. ON these two commandments hang all the law and the prophets"**. [Hebrews 11:6] **"------: for he that cometh to God must believe that he is and that he is a rewarder of them that diligently seek him."** This **"diligently seeking God" is accomplished by "studying, loving, delighting in and meditating in God's Word to show thyself approved unto God, [Acts 2:4] gladly receiving his word and [Deuteronomy 28:47] serving the Lord thy God with joyfulness and gladness of heart for the abundance of all things."** Maintaining a proper Bible conditioned attitude is vitally essential through all this.

Just do it and, to be sure, your wisdom will increase as will your understanding, knowledge, intelligence, and discretion in the use of God's Word. You will be amazed at how things pertaining to plain old fashioned "common sense" will emerge as you explore the depths of God's counsel and direction. Other "essentials" will come into focus, take their proper places, and contribute to your growth, development and maturity in Christ, **"for it is the doers of the word, not the hearers only that are justified in God's sight", [Romans 2: 13].**

In the instruction, guidance, and counsel of God's word for the development of a life and life more abundantly, you will find nothing that could be classified as a non-essential for your advancement unto perfection and maturity in Christ. Even what we might consider as suggestions from God are important enough for us to view as commands whereby we may profit and advance in our journey of life. If we can become more concerned about designing our time and life in doing always those things that please God by cleaning up our thinking and thoughts, **[Isaiah 55: 8-9], "For my thoughts are not your thoughts, neither are your ways my ways, saith the Lord. For as the heavens are higher than the earth, so are my ways higher than your ways, and my thoughts than your thoughts",** we will find that we naturally tend to draw away from and resist the temptations and transgressions that cause us so many problems and grieve the Holy Spirit. This will be greatly facilitated by embracing **[Colossians 3: 2], "Set your affection on things above, not on things on the earth".** It does take time and some determination to learn to **[Proverbs 4: 23], "Keep thy heart with all diligence; for out of it are the issues of life".** Learn what the essentials are, get a vision of the value of them and establish them in your life.

NOTES

IV. WAY, TRUTH, LIFE

[John 14:6],"Jesus saith unto him, I am the way, the truth, and the life: no man cometh unto the Father but by me". There is coming a time when man will realize his folly of considering science, as he understands it, to be the standard by which all things are to be measured, accepted and or rejected. The scorners, scoffers and all others who fit in the category of opposition to God, who claim there is no scientific evidence to prove there is a God, have, themselves, offered no scientific evidence or proof to the contrary. So they continue to rail against the truth of the gospel in their efforts to prove nothing of value. I see this as only a feeble attempt to defend their own pointless position of Godlessness and unbelief, a position that provides nothing of value for the adherents in the process of believing it, and no rewards or benefits in the final culmination of all things. It is a dead end street with nothing there but hopelessness, failure, and death when you finely arrive. The only point is something to argue about in an effort to attempt an end run around God; to go where?

If, in the course of their argument, they convince someone to "diversify" in their direction, what have they accomplished but to recruit another blind follower that may give them a little satisfaction and company, as together they deceive and encourage each other onward into the ditch of destruction, **[Matthew 23: 15], "Woe unto you, scribes and Pharisees, hypocrites! For ye compass sea and land to make one proselyte, and when he is made, ye make him twofold more the child of hell than yourselves".[Matthew 15:13-14], "But he answered and said, Every plant, which my heavenly Father hath not planted shall be rooted up. Let them alone: they be blind leaders of the blind, And if the blind lead the blind, both shall fall into the ditch".** "Let them alone": it seems to be an exhortation to not waste your time on them as, **[Proverbs 1:7], "The fear of the Lord is the beginning of knowledge: but fools despise wisdom and instruction".** There are many scriptures in Proverbs, indeed the Bible, that speak of people such as this, that tell where they come from, whose leading them, and certainly where they are headed. Their way is not the way of Jesus. **[Isaiah 55: 6-9], "Seek ye the Lord while he may be found, call ye upon him while he is near; Let the wicked, those conformed to the world, forsake his way, and the unrighteous man his thoughts: and let him return unto the Lord, for he will abundantly pardon. For my thoughts are not your thoughts, neither are your ways my ways, saith the Lord. For as the heavens are higher than the earth, so are my ways higher than your ways, and my thoughts than your thoughts".**

There is a saying that has considerable creditability, **"If you continue to think the way you've always thought, you'll continue to get what you've always got".** The reason it has such credibility is simply because it reflects Biblical principle and truth. **[Proverbs 23:7] "For as he thinketh in his heart, so is he: Eat and drink saith he to thee, but his heart is not with thee".** This deceptive condition of the heart as recorded is comparative to that recorded in **[Matthew 15:8; Mark 7:6], "This people draweth nigh unto me with their mouth and hounoreth me with their lips, but their heart is far from me".**

This deception and making of lies is a common condition among humanity in our world today, making its arrogant appearance throughout our judicial and governmental systems continually. This is a very interesting portion of scripture. What he said revealed the deceptive WAY that was the thinking of his heart, which in this case may well be considered his mind as they are synonymous in situations and conditions such as this.

The solution and correction for this is found in scriptures such as **[Proverbs 4:23], "Keep thy heart [mind] with all diligence; for out of it are the issues [ways] of life." This is referring to the "heart that is kept with all diligence", nourished and developed in the wisdom, knowledge, and, understanding, of God's righteous counsel, the Bible.**

The heart that is not "diligently kept, nourished, and developed in this "word of life" brings forth, issues [ways] of death, such as the deceptive condition of the heart in [Proverbs 23:7] above. It would be fitting to include here a companion scripture, **[Romans 12:2]** for the renewing of the mind unto Biblical truths, absolutes, principles and counsel for the delivering of the entire being from conformity to the world and its destructive results. This conformity to the world is the prevailing way that we see evidence of continually in our own nation, practiced in a multitude of ways by our "own countrymen". I sometimes wonder if it wouldn't be appropriate in the evidence of such a huge abundance of these devious ways, scams, to add a "Sc" on the front of America. Lies and deceptions have made many inroads into our American society and culture in our post modern era and come under the heading of **"inventors of evil things", [Romans 1:30].**

It grieves me to think that conditions are such in our grand nation as to even warrant such an idea, but with the multitudes of new scams being tried continually, it does seem to fit. The life is consistently being drained out of America because of her increasing abominations and iniquities, **"[Hosea 4:6-7], verse 7 "As they increased so they sinned against me: therefore I will change their glory into shame".** It would seem that America is reaping as she has sown in her excommunicating of God and despising his word. Man does have the propensity to not only mess in his own nest, but to mess it up everyone else's as well, and condition others to the same erroneous ways.

[1Corinthians 5:6-7; Galatians 5:9], Of a truth, **"a little leaven leaveneth the whole lump"**, especially if it is the old leaven of sin that compliments the evil nature that we were all born with, that even when cast out has a tendency to lurk around in the shadows waiting for an opportunity to reassert itself, which we at times of ignorance and stupidity offer it. Indeed Mr. Shakespeare, "What fools we mortals have continued to be", therefore, **[1Peter 5:8], "Be sober, be vigilant; because your adversary the devil, as a roaring lion, walketh about, seeking whom he may devour"**, and rest assured, *he knows where you live.* Thus we are admonished, even as Christians, to **[Colossians 3:2] "Set your affection on things above, not on things on the earth"**. These things "above" are the ways of truth and life that produce ways of truth and life here below, lifestyles with hearts and minds that issue forth ways of truth and life, versus the ways of the world from deceptive hearts and minds that issue forth ways of additional deception, deceit, and death.

[Romans 12:1-2], "I beseech you therefore, brethren, by the mercies of God, that ye present your bodies a living sacrifice, holy, acceptable unto God, which is your reasonable service. And be not conformed to [the ways of] this world: but be ye transformed by the renewing of your mind that ye may prove what is that good, and acceptable, and perfect will of God". This good, and acceptable, and perfect will of God is a brief description of God's ways, which are prompted and set in motion according to God's thoughts and thinking; which thoughts, and thinking, we are to learn about, and practice in order to emulate his ways, preventing being devoured by the adversary. These ways are, of course, **"the way and the truth, and the life" of which Jesus is the living manifestation, and perfect example.** It is easy to talk about this, read about it, and hear others preach and teach on these things. The rub comes in learning and blending our lives into them and becoming one with them as Jesus himself is. **These things" are the things that always please God, [John 8:29] and the things that accompany salvation, [Hebrews 6:9]**, an accumulation of which is found throughout God's word. How do we find out about these "things"? There is an interesting concept we find in the Bible called **[2 Timothy 2:15], "STUDY" to show thyself approved into God, a workman that needeth not to be ashamed, rightly dividing the word of truth"**. "STUDY" to fill your heart and being with an abundance of God's counsel of righteousness, the knowledge of the Lord that prevents destruction. STUDY, that's how we find out about these **"things"**.

In **[Psalms 1:2]** there are some additional ideas that should help the interested student to proceed in his pursuit of Godly counsel, **"But his delight is in the law, word, of the Lord; and in his word doth he meditate day and night"**. **[Psalms 119:165]** gives us an interesting reason for "loving" the word of God. If we take, loving, delighting in and meditating on, the word of God for the purpose of "doing always those things that please God" in obedience for service to him, with joyfulness and gladness of heart, rest assured we will enjoy the abundance of all things, [Deuteronomy 28:47], for God is indeed a rewarder of them that diligently seek him. [Hebrews 11:6], "But without faith it is impossible to please him: for he that cometh to God must believe that he is, and that he is a rewarder of them that diligently seek him"**. His rewards are of a great abundance for those who meet the requirements of being a faithful believer that God is; and that the method of seeking him is with DILIGENCE, **"serving him with joyfulness and gladness of heart for the abundance of all things', [Deuteronomy 28: 47]**.

NOTES

V. RIGHTLY DIVIDING THE WORD OF TRUTH

[2 Timothy 2:15], "Study to show thyself approved unto God, a workman that needeth not to be ashamed, RIGHTLY DIVIDING THE WORD OF TRUTH". [John 8: 31-32], "Then Jesus said to those Jews, or whoever, that believe on him, If ye continue in my word, THEN are ye my disciples indeed". If a person is to continue in the "word of truth", there must be a beginning before there can be a continuing. We find this beginning **in [Matthew 17:5, Mark 9:7, John 9:35], "While he yet spoke, behold a bright cloud overshadowed them: and a voice out of the cloud, which said, This is my beloved Son in whom I am well pleased; HEAR YE HIM". In [James 1:21-25] we get necessary insight into this handling of the word. Vs. 22, "But be ye DOERS of the word, not hearers only, deceiving your own selves".** Let us pick up another scripture, there are others, for further instruction into this area of consideration and study, **[Romans 2:13], "For not the hearers of the law, word, are just before God, but the DOERS of the law, word, shall be justified".** I see a need to insert the word "word" here in place of "law' as a lot of people have a real problem with this thing of law versus grace, and there is a real need to study to **"rightly divide the word of truth"** in this area.

Law and grace are both to be found in both Old and New Testaments in their own areas, but the "Word" includes and covers them both wherever or whenever they appear and the consideration is applicable. **[Psalms 119]** is a good example of this where several words are used with all of them referring directly to the "word". It is up to us to search out and apply the proper understanding in all areas. Herein we find the need to **"study to show our selves approved unto God",** fulfilling our individual calling, whatever it may be. Regardless, studying to be a doer of the word and not a hearer only is essential in all areas whereunto we may be called, privileged, and honored to serve our God and our Lord Jesus Christ. It is important for us to realize and remember that God has provided an abundance of all things for those who **"serve him with joyfulness and gladness of heart", [Deuteronomy 28:47].** There are many blessings, things that are of a general abundance for all men, but there are specifics that extend beyond these that are enjoyed only by those **willing servants who love and reverence God, keeping their hearts with all diligence, loving and meditating in the word day and night, and studying to show themselves approved unto God,** *"rightly dividing the word of truth",* **[2 Timothy 2: 15].**

This all begins with **[Mark1:15], "Repent ye and believe the gospel"** unto obedience and continuing as we are instructed in **[Matthew 6:33], "Seek ye first the kingdom of God and his righteousness and all these things shall be added unto you".** This is one of the **"great and precious promises" spoken of in [2 Peter1: 4].** First we have the command to **"Seek ye first he kingdom of God and his righteousness"**, then we have the promise of the result; or "effect" of the "cause", being obedient, **"and all these things shall be added unto you".** We might see these situations as "cause and effect". Obedience to the command which holds the promise, the cause, the result is the effect. Be disobedient to the commands, the principles, the word, and I assure you, there are different promises that will apply to you whether you like it or not, and the result and effect will be considerably different and undesirable. Don't blame God for the adverse effects you bring down on your own head by your rebellion and disobedience.

There are other promises that take place in the cases of disobedience. Study **[Deuteronomy 28]** to get an in depth look at the results and effects of the cause for both obedience and disobedience. Though this was originally given to the Hebrews millennia ago, but the principles have not changed nor diminished. **[Roman 6:23], "The wages of sin is still death; but for the redeemed, the gift of God through Jesus Christ is still, and forever will be life and life more abundantly". [2 Corinthians 1:20], "For all the promises of God in him [Jesus Christ], are yea, and in him Amen, unto the glory of God by us".** Study **[Ezekiel 18]** and see the majesty of God in his love, mercy, grace, and forgiveness, toward the wicked who, with the whole heart, turn from their wicked ways in repentance and embrace the truth and counsel of the Lord in willing, joyful, obedience, loving his word, revering and loving God, and working righteousness, **[Acts 10: 34-35].** In this same chapter, **Ezekiel 18,** it is also found that the responsibility for sin rests on the one who commits such sin **regardless of how he was taught.** The only responsibility the parent teacher has, and it is a tremendous responsibility and privilege, in this area is to **[Proverbs 22:6], "Train up a child in the way he should go, to establish the principles of life and obedience within that child, [Deuteronomy 4:9; 5:9-10; 6:7; 7:9;].**

However, failing to fulfill the responsibilities, obligations, duties, and privileges of a parent, teacher, leader, and provider, which includes many things beyond food, clothing, and shelter; brings about temporal, generational, and eternal consequences and effects based on the failure, the cause. How that child eventually turns out is his own responsibility, it is "upon his own head". He must make his own decisions and choices, *but we must give them the benefit of proper Bible orientated counsel and conditioning,* so that when they are old they will not depart from it, or as the prodigal son, at least "come to himself" and return to it. They may take some bumps and bruises along the way, but like the prodigal son when degraded into keeping company with the swine of this world, **[Matthew 7:6],** yet supported by much prayer, will remember his Fathers house wherein he was loved, raised, taught, and nourished, and return to it; probably a bit more humble than when he left, but nevertheless, home.

[Ephesians 2:1-3], We all have had our turn at "prodigalism" in one way or another, or to one degree or another and have taken some lumps for our transgressions; indeed the way of the transgressor is hard as well as deadly. **Verse 4, But God, But God,** this majestic, loving, intervening God interrupts our waywardness and intervenes on our behalf, **verses 4-10.** He may have to take us to the "wood shed" from time to time to apply the board of education for corrective measures to the seat of the problem, but, that's only showing his love and concern for our well being and soul prosperity for eternity. Otherwise, without this stern correction, we remain, **"by nature, the children of wrath, even as others" vs. 3, corrupt trees bearing evil fruit, good for nothing but to be cut down and cast into the fire, [Matthew 7:17-20]. [Ephesians 2: 4], "But God, who is rich in mercy, for his great love wherein he loved us------".**

The responsibility and obligation of "rightly dividing the word of truth" is in itself a tremendous challenge demanding the "study" commanded and necessary to do so. It comes from the Gr. "orthotomeo", meaning to set straight, or to handle right and correctly. It may be looked at as rightly dissecting and the correct expounding of the various applications and meanings of words. This involves much more study than most people are willing to commit themselves to; nor do they see the value, benefits, and rewards of such commitment in receiving additional wisdom, the gaining of understanding, and the advancement of knowledge. According to **[Hosea 4: 6]** this knowledge is what prevents our destruction.

Personally I see great value in this, of course having the knowledge needed to prevent destruction is one thing, having the intelligence and common sense to use it is entirely another. These are all wonderful "effects", resulting from the cause, "study". This will only be accomplished as people indulge themselves in intense study and meditation concerning these matters, **[Philippians 4:8; Psalms 1:2].** This intense study and meditation will only occur as we exercise ourselves to get a vision of the value of such intense study and meditation. An in-depth analysis of the benefits of the results and effects may prompt an inducement toward such study and meditation.

Intelligence or common sense, either one will direct our efforts in this direction. By God's grace we find that salvation is not contingent on knowing these things, but is based on **[Mark 1:15], repentance from sin, and believing the gospel unto salvation.** The requirements for believing the gospel unto salvation, as essential as they are, are considerably less than the requirements for believing and studying unto the gaining of wisdom, knowledge, understanding, and the intelligence that embraces and promotes willing obedience unto righteousness.

These are among the **"things that accompany salvation", [Hebrews 6:9],** which involves a lifetime of learning and developing. Unfortunately, there has been a lack of teaching on the subject of "believing" and the different levels or depths of it. We find this in the application of **[Acts 16:13], "Believe on the Lord Jesus Christ and thou shalt be saved, and thy house".**

The concept of believing here involves the embracing of, and *doing*, being obedient to the gospel, which begins with heart depth acknowledging and repentance of sin, **[Mark 1: 15],** which is seldom taught and explained as a necessity for putting the life under **the "cleansing blood of Jesus", [1John 1:7-8], "If we say we have fellowship with him, but remain**

unrepentant, and walk in darkness, we lie, and do not the truth: But if we "repent", and walk in the light, as he is the light, we have fellowship one with another, and the blood of Jesus Christ his Son cleanseth us from ALL SIN". [John 3:7], "Ye must be born again". [John 15:3], "Now ye are clean through the [applied] word that I have spoken unto you".

The application of this word is absolutely essential in the continuation of the cleansing process of remaining clean. Spiritual development and maturing unto a good tree producing good fruit for God's glory and honour is not an automatic thing just because you raised your hand to accept Jesus as your Lord and Saviour. Neither do you receive a degree just because you registered in the first grade. There are some things required to advance as a successful student and there are things that are required to accompany salvation, **[Hebrews 6:9]; that it, salvation, might take root and "bring forth fruit meet for repentance", [Matthew 3:8],** and in repenting and turning to God, **doing works meet for repentance,** which prove that true repentance from sin has taken place in the heart, **[Acts 26:20].** If this is not done; we have many professing Christianity who are characterized in **[Matthew 15:8; Mark 7:6].**

These spend much time in counseling sessions trying to find out why they are having the problems they are experiencing in their attempts to integrate the impurities of being unrepentant with the requirement of repentance from such foolishness. These are those who have mouthed an acceptance of Jesus but keep one foot firmly planted in the "if it feels good, do it" system of this world and, and as a result, have a great tendency to blame God for their problems, never learning that **"it is the goodness of God that leads to true repentance", [Romans 2:4].** To diligently follow the leading of the Holy Spirit in obedience of God's word and counsel is the absolute necessity for salvation and bearing of good fruit.

It is obvious that not all people come to the same conclusions in the process of **"rightly dividing the word of truth"**, even within Christendom, the result being the many different denominations as evidenced. Even within the various denominations, you will find separations into different divisions with variations of doctrinal beliefs. Unfortunately this gives rise to church, or denominational, doctrine, in many cases, becoming more of a concern and more important to "believers" than Biblical doctrine.

Because of this, we are witnessing today in some movements, sin and its practice, not being viewed as sin to be repented of, but a matter of constitutional rights to be indulged in. God is no longer regarded as God, to be reverenced, loved, honored, glorified, praised, and obeyed, but to be dismissed as irrelevant and non-essential, whose word is neither important nor relative to today's world. Of course if you excommunicate God, cast away, and despise his word of truth, then there is no longer a need to "rightly divide his word of truth" and the transgressors can foolishly and blissfully go tiptoeing through the willful ignorance of their existence congratulating themselves on their accomplishments of self- deliverance; until_____!

[Isaiah 5:20], "Woe unto them that call evil good, and good evil; that put darkness for light, and light for darkness; that put bitter for sweet and sweet for bitter"; [Galatians 6:7], "Be not deceived; God is not mocked: for whatsoever a man soweth, that shall he also reap". Be assured, these are also promises of God. All will come to pass in their appropriate times; whether good or evil, blessing or cursing, and every person will receive unto themselves that which they have chosen, **therefore choose life that both you and your "seed", descendents shall live, [Deuteronomy 30:19], [Hebrews 2: 2-3].**

There is no doubt that people endowed with at least the minimum intelligence required considering the alternative of death and cursing, will make the correct choice of life and blessing, even if it were based only on a possibility of it coming to pass. Whether the contrary, worldly, alternative was to prove viable or not; just the choice of it constitutes disaster for all involved. **[James 4:4], "Ye adulterers and adulteresses, know ye not that the friendship of the world is enmity with God? Whosoever therefore will be a friend of the world is the enemy of God".**

There are many things other than adultery to be considered here. Let us consider these deluded souls that are of the world, thus enemies of God. As they have chosen this world as their home, doesn't it seem that they would attempt to take better care of it? However, that would be impossible without submitting to God in order to resist the devil and causing him to flee from them, thus releasing themselves to the counsel and wisdom of God to guide and direct them. **[James 4:7], "Submit yourselves therefore to God. Resist the devil and he will flee from you".**

Here we are seeing commands and promises, causes and effects at work again. First, the command or cause, **"Submit yourselves therefore to God, and, second, resist the devil. You must do the first before it is possible to do the second. Then we see the promise and effect, taking place, "and he, the devil, will flee from you".**

I don't know how many times I have heard people, including Christians, say; Resist the devil and he will flee from you, without emphasizing or even mentioning the first command to submit themselves to God which makes it all possible. We see a rather vivid accounting of attempting to resist the devil with out submission to God in **[Acts 19:13-16]**. However the Bible has recorded multitudes, and the world is full people who have been devoured by this one who goes about as a roaring lion, **[1Peter 5:8]**, who make no pretense of resisting him, but instead, assist him in his evil work in all manner of iniquity.

It seems that there is no end to the time, effort, and expense that people will go to in embracing their choice of death and cursing with the same ignorant reasoning that is so typical of this worlds mentality, "I've got my rights". I must mention here again, a quote of William Shakespeare's, **"What fools ye mortals be"**. Amen Willie; well said. We can see the Bible equivalent of this in **[Proverbs 1:7], "The fear of the Lord is the beginning of knowledge: but fools despise wisdom and instruction"**, and so we see our world, and our nation, in the condition they are in and steadily getting worse, it seems, on a daily basis; without people reverencing God to even show and interest in, nor getting started on, the beginning of the knowledge needed to avert destruction, **[Hosea 4:6]**.

It seems we have multitudes of leaders in all areas that don't even have a clue about Godly wisdom or Biblical instruction in **"the knowledge of the holy which is understanding"**, **[Proverbs 9:10].** *As a consequence they do not have the requirements, wisdom, understanding, knowledge, and it seems, the basic intelligence and common sense necessary to lead the nation in righteousness, nor do they have the will*. As a result, they don't even encourage it, but to the contrary forbid it because these things are taught in the Bible, which is the foundation of the Christian religion, which of course is connected to church.

All this becomes forbidden under the erroneous "separation of church and state" nonsense, which seems to be aimed at, and peculiar to the Christian faith, or religion, the foundation, strength, and direction of America. So in **despising these things of God and casting them away,** we see our nation locked into a self-destruct mode by the foolishness of mortals, not only in leadership positions but all areas of our once great nation, from the least to the greatest. It never ceases to amaze me how Americans can continue to wallow in the sea of iniquity they have devised in their rebellion against God and then have the gall to sing "God Bless America" as if to expect him to bless and reward them for their disobedience and abominations.

It seems that the foolishness of *"ye mortals"* intensifies continually and the "whole land is made desolate" of the knowledge of God and his righteousness; because of the lack and execution of the Godly qualities of wisdom, knowledge, understanding, and yes, intelligence and common sense, **[Jeremiah 4: 19-27; 12: 9-13]. [Hosea 4: 6-7], "My people are destroyed for lack of knowledge: because thou hast rejected knowledge, I will also reject thee that thou shalt be no priest to me: seeing thou hast forgotten the law of thy God, I will also forget thy children. As they were increased, so they sinned against me: therefore I will change their glory into shame".**

From the present condition of America, I would have to conclude that we are witnessing today, our glory being turned into shame, and who's to **blame but those who sin against God, casting his word behind their backs and despising it, [Isaiah 5:12-13], "but they regard not the work of the Lord, neither consider the operation of his hands, therefore my people are gone into captivity, because they have no knowledge: and their honorable men are famished, and their multitude dried up with thirst; vs. 24, "because they** have cast away the law, statutes, commandments, truth, of the Lord of hosts, and despised the word of the Holy One of Israel".

It is true that Israel was the people being immediately addressed here, but we must look beyond that to the principles that were being initiated and established by God for the well being and good of all men everywhere. We find this principle of obedience with the resultant blessings specifically stated in **[Deuteronomy 10: 12-13].** Now how would it apply if we were to substitute "America" for Israel at the beginning of verse 12? To take it a bit further, try substituting your own name and see if it fits. Then see if you can find some additional scriptures that will support this principle with its commands "for thy good". Try **[Deuteronomy 30:19-20],** there are many others. This is a worthwhile exercise that will keep you busy for awhile, and produce wonderful benefits. In this search for additional scriptures you may be amazed at the things you will stumble over that have been before you all the time that will also be **"for thy good".**

God has never established and designed anything that was not for our benefit and promotion unto righteousness. All he has ever done, is doing, and will continue to do is for our good to bring us to repentance, redemption, and reconciliation. His love for his creation would not allow him to do less. This same love must be alive in our hearts in compelling and motivating us to also conduct ourselves according to the demands of such love, as good trees producing good fruit, embracing and doing those things that accompany salvation with the resultant lifestyle, and doing always those things that are acceptable to God and please him. **[Philippians 4:7-9], "Think on these things and the peace of God which passeth understanding, shall keep your hearts and minds through Christ Jesus",** Amen.

NOTES

VI. SET IN HIS WAYS

[Isaiah 55:8]; "For my thoughts are not your thoughts, neither are your ways my ways, saith the Lord". I have heard it said, when I was younger, that people become set in their ways especially as they get older. I have found this to be true now that, I too through no choice of my own am getting older, which is considerably better than the inevitable alternative. This "older thing" does have some tremendous benefits, however if as we grow older, if we become vividly conscious of the fact that growing as you get older has greater significance than just getting older. We are all getting older, but are we growing as we get older? This has nothing to do with your wardrobe seeming to shrink as the later years seem to stalk us as a predator stalks its prey which has no hope of escape. But, however, if we were to replace prey with pray we find that the predator has lost **"both its sting and its victory", [1 Corinthians. 15:55].**

So, what is the difference between getting older and growing older? Maturity in Christ; and what a glorious difference it is: this continuing to grow as we get older. Have you, or are you becoming set in your ways? This has some very severe implications that we need to be aware of as it is the ways that follow the thinking and thoughts that we establish over a period of time, which if incorrect according to Biblical teaching, have a strong tendency to form some very destructive habits that in many cases become the lifestyle and, if not corrected become the destiny of ultimate destruction. Getting older is inevitable, but growing older is a choice, maturing in Christ is a conscious choice that must be made for our benefit, for our children's benefit, for societies benefit, and most important for God's benefit, the bringing of pleasure to his heart. The establishment of a God pleasing culture is of extreme importance and it must begin as a personal development to render unto God his rights to receive from us that which is due him as GOD.

God's rights: now there's and interesting thought and area to explore. We've never thought or heard anything about God's rights. I guess man has been to busy about the selfish business of establishing his own personal self declared rights and making everyone around him aware of the fact that he has them. These are the people that only get older and have not learned how to grow older. Unfortunately many of them get older at a younger age for lack of spiritual maturity. **[Hosea 4:6], "My people are destroyed for lack of knowledge".** There is much more to this scripture than is stated here. I would encourage the reader to study the remainder of it and take it to heart.

This can and does take place at any age. It doesn't have to wait until the "golden years" arrive. The fact is, if spiritual maturity is not established in the younger years, the "golden years" may lack much of the gold, materially and spiritually that is necessary to make them "golden". **[Psalms 111:10] "The fear, revering, of God is the beginning of wisdom and, [Proverbs 1:7] the beginning of knowledge". [Proverbs 4:7], "Wisdom is the principal thing; therefore get wisdom: and with all thy getting get understanding".** So we have **wisdom, understanding, and knowledge** which give us God's counsel and direction to mature and grow into. To just get older without attaining to these Godly provisions is to just exist without really understanding what living is all about. These are among the "things that accompany salvation" **[Hebrews 6: 9],** that are of the great treasures of which life consists. These are of the main items which **"the thief cometh not, but for to steal, and to kill, and to destroy", [John 10: 10].** They are also essential to the **"life and life more abundantly that Jesus came to give us".**

Wisdom, knowledge, and understanding; the three main ingredients of which life is comprised! Without them man becomes as a **"whited sepulcher, which indeed appears beautiful outward, but are within full of dead men's bones, and of all uncleanness"**, [Matthew 24: 27]. These three essentials, without a doubt are all inclusive of God's thoughts, and thus determine his ways. I am inclined to believe these are part of that of which God was referring to when he told Adam in **[Genesis 2: 17], "But of the tree of the knowledge of good and evil, thou shalt not eat of it,** *for in the day thou eatest thereof thou shalt surely die".*

The very thought of disobedience itself showed a complete absence of wisdom and this same deficiency of thought has been plaguing man every since. It is introduced to us again in its original setting concerning Lucifer [Satan] in **[Ezekiel 28: 12-19]**, see vs. 15, **"Thou wast perfect in thy ways from the day that thou wast created,** *till* iniquity *was found in thee".* So even Satan became set in his ways of iniquity because of his thinking and thoughts of iniquity completely void of wisdom and intelligence, and man continues to be set in his ways of iniquity for the same reasons. Man doesn't seem to be able to come up with the knowledge to understand that if his ways are going to change he has to have a renewing of his thoughts and thinking, his mindset, **[Romans 12: 2]**. So he continues to struggle along in his ignorance and **"lack of knowledge, being destroyed" [Hosea 4: 6-7], and reaping shame** for his sowing of seeds of stupidity in his heart and mind. He was perfect in his ways, being created in the image and likeness of God, **until iniquity was found in him,** then he too become set in his pernicious ways.

These things certainly give us valuable insight into the thinking, thoughts and ways of God and a challenge to explore his intelligence concerning the need for us to attain to these areas of thought and thinking. We might, if we are awake and honest with ourselves, find some areas here in which we are lacking. What a glorious revelation that would be. What a wonderful change in our lives would be wrought if we would learn to adopt his line of thinking so that our thoughts would become blended into his thoughts and our ways would become "set" in God's ways, **[2 Corinthians 10:5], "Casting down imaginations, and every high thing that exalts itself against the knowledge of God, and bringing very thought to the obedience of Christ".** If we will discipline ourselves to think God's thoughts, **[Philippians 4: 8-9],** then we will be able to become **"set in his ways",** becoming a positive part of his eternal agenda.

NOTES

NOTES

VII. THE ENEMY WITHIN

If you continue to think the way you've always thought, you'll continue to get what you've always got. That is precisely why America is not getting what she used to get: because she doesn't think the way she used to think. It is true that America is not without some dark places in her history, but there was, in the past, even among many who didn't claim to be Christians, a much greater respect for the Bible and the Christian faith or "religion" as some would call it. There were some Biblical truths and absolutes in place, respected and taught by some people that were not even committed Christians, and the influence of these things was even manifested in the major portion of our judicial system as well as throughout our political ranks. The intrinsic value contained within these Biblically presented, God originated absolutes of eternal truths were seen even by many common men on the fringes of the Christian lifestyle as basic to the needs of our America's beginning and her successful continuation.

Had we the caliber of leaders today that our nation had in her beginnings, men of Biblical convictions for the needs and requirements of these Godly principles for the establishment of America, and led and emphasized among the populace the need for these principles, we would be living in a much improved nation. However, the way they thought concerning those needs was lost when our "founding fathers" passed on into history and the modernists, the next generation who knew not, what God had done for America took charge. It is questionable as to whether or not they even cared: our most recent "leaders" certainly don't seem to. The whole scenario is somewhat akin to a situation we find in **[Judges 2: 7-10], "vs. 7, And the people served the Lord all the days of Joshua, and all the days of** the elders that outlived Joshua, *who had seen the great works of the Lord, that he did for Israel.* Then Joshua died and was buried, vss, 8-9. **[Verse 10], And also all that generation were gathered unto their fathers,** *died*: **and there arose another generation,** *modernists, relativists, secularists, ACLU, ETC, ETC,* **after them, which knew not the Lord, nor the works that he had done for Israel [America].** Isn't it amazing how history does repeat itself? Verse 11 continues, **"And the children Israel,** or America, whichever the case may be, **did evil in the sight of the Lord, and served the gods of political correctness, diversity, liberalism, secularism, materialism, and constitutional rights based on this worlds wisdom, etc, etc.**

Today we have many who, though professing Christianity, show little concern for many of the basic, fundamental Bible principles which did, in fact, form the foundation on which America was built and in which she was anchored. Neither is this in its entirety nor in part, taught in our schools today. Unfortunately we have many within our governing structures today, taught as the *"higher powers"* from [**Romans 13:1**], who are instrumental in ripping the moorings of our nation loose from our ancient God given, Bible based foundation and security. Assisting them in this national demise and destruction are many anti-God, anti-Bible, and as a result, anti-American groups and organizations including a government that has been instrumental in excommunicating God and His word. And any attempt to reverse this travesty of justice, good, and righteousness, is branded as illegal and politically incorrect.

Our young people are exiting America's educational institutions without any taught, or learned, knowledge, care, or concern about the values of this God or his ordained foundation of the nation where they hope to build their futures. This has virtually been destroyed because of governmental imposition of the "separation of church and state nonsense. Thus has the state, instead of fulfilling their God ordained obligations, duties and responsibilities, to God and the good of the nation blocked the avenue of God's Word of direction and hope, but have become guilty of war against God and his kingdom. Incompetent, inept, and corrupt leadership has destroyed many nations, and it appears that America is on the list.

Because of this our nation has become terribly confused and divided, and the "American dream" is a myth that is rapidly exploding in the faces of our young people. Consequently, without these God given values firmly anchored within their hearts and minds as their own personal foundation on which to build their lives, they have no hope or future; and we are consistently seeing graphic signs and evidences of their increasing frustration and hopelessness surfacing in their self destructing behavior. Such valueless behavior is not only destroying themselves, but those around them; and their nation has taught them this as being a constitutional right, and "being free", the result of the "if it feels good, do it" philosophy that has invaded our American culture and is wreaking such havoc among us.

We are indeed "the enemy within", maybe not perpetrating these evils, but neither doing what is necessary to prevent and alleviate them either. What absolute ridiculous idiocy has been fed to our people that has eliminated the essential teachings and knowledge that is necessary to the building of Godly character for the wellbeing of all: including our America. Such is the condition of this God blessed country that our children are inheriting, that their ancestors, certainly including their parents, should never have allowed to digress to its present condition of sinfulness. As an adult Christian, I feel the need to apologize to our young people for handing over to them as their inheritance, such a beleaguered, indebted, sin ridden, mess, and expect them to straighten it out. **[Galatians 6:7-8], "Be not deceived; God is not mocked: for whatsoever a man [or a nation] soweth, that shall he [it] also reap. For he that soweth to his flesh shall of the flesh reap corruption; but he that soweth to the Spirit shall of the Spirit reap life everlasting".**

Without the governing direction of a Biblical foundation to support a nation, that nation will immediately begin to weaken and eventually disappear, appearing only in history books, providing any are even written in the future. When the concept of "the separation of church and state" was illegally slipped into the constitution and imposed on the American scene, God and His Word were excommunicated by governmental decree. False religions were then allowed to impose themselves on America by constitutional directive of the "freedom of religion", and the Bible foundation and support was cast aside and has nearly been destroyed, and without the wherewithal to preserve and maintain it, we are suffering horribly as a result. So much for the wisdom and guidance of the *"higher powers"* and the mentality that allowed the establishment of these pseudo authorities!

If the church can ever come to the realization that these *"higher powers"* are elements of God's divine nature to which all men must subject themselves for the sake of unity and being "seated together in heavenly places in Christ Jesus for the glory of God and prosperity of his creation, then we will experience a wonder to behold among us. If they don't, we can expect things to continue to as they are, in demise and degradation, **[Isaiah 5: 24], "Therefore as the fire devoureth the stubble, and the flame consumeth the chaff, so their root shall be as rottenness, and their blossom shall go up as dust: because they have cast away the law of the Lord of hosts, and despised the word of the Holy One of Israel".**

We have much historical information today that testifies to that fact of nations, past and present, and world wide, that have victimized themselves by their unscrupulous idiocy and overwhelming stupidity. And America's leaders, her so called "higher powers??" are taking her increasingly in the same direction. When the essential thinking of the leadership of a nation becomes opposed to the God of creation and departs from his counsel and guidance, that nation, with a few individuals who as exceptions hold to Biblical truths and absolutes, will fall.

Today we are experiencing the demise of the greatest nation this world has ever known because her leadership and majority have **[Isaiah 5:24] "cast away the law, WORD, of the Lord of hosts and despised the word of the Holy One of Israel"**. As a result of this idiocy of transgression against God, we are experiencing the first part of this scripture: **"Therefore as the fire devoureth the stubble, and the flame consumeth the chaff, so their root shall be as rottenness, and their "blossom" [children] shall go up as dust"**. Verse 25 can also be applied here in principle as part of the curse America has brought on herself through disobedience and rebellion; the affects of which we are seeing everyday and don't have the sense or ability to correct: **[2 Chronicles 7: 14], "If my people, which are called by my name, shall humble themselves, and pray, and seek my face, and turn from their wicked ways; THEN will I hear from heaven, and will forgive their sin, and will heal their land"**. It is going to take leaders and the led both together to initiate this, but with their self imposed barriers of selfishness and pride, it is doubtful it will happen.

With the initiating of erroneous thinking in opposition to the word of God through the leadership and so called judicial authorities in sneaking in this wrongly imposed "separation of church and state" nonsense into our constitution, they have essentially choked off God's influence to America. These are spoken of in **[Romans 1:18], "for the wrath of God is revealed from heaven against all ungodliness and unrighteousness of men, who hold, [suppress, imprison, and bridle] the truth in unrighteousness."**

This evil pattern of opposition and rebellion to God and his word has become a set condition in the hearts of a contrary majority, many who are charged, as leaders, with the responsibility of national safety, security, strength and guidance. These have become, because of their erroneous condition of heart and mind, "the enemy within", the bearers of "evil fruit", "our own countrymen", opposing themselves, and bringing destruction on all that come within their sphere of influence; that which has been entrusted to them for their care, enrichment, development, and protection. May God have mercy on us, and forgive us for being so stupid as to allow such stupidity to become the norm and characterize America. We get an accurate description of our national condition from **[Matthew 23: 28], "Even so ye also outwardly appear righteous unto men, but within ye are full of hypocrisy and iniquity"**. The exterior appearance of righteousness has, to an overwhelming extent, also disappeared. **[Job 4: 21], "Doth not their excellency which is in them go away? They die, even without wisdom"**, *the very beginning of which, is the fear, the reverence, of God,* **[Psalms 111: 10; Proverbs 1: 7; 9: 10]**.

It makes no difference that they were born in this nation and are legal citizens and would undoubtedly declare themselves as loyal Americans and staunch patriots. They nevertheless, in their wickedness of mentality and spirit are blind leaders, who in their deception create many blind followers, all headed for the ditch of destruction and taking America with them. **[Luke 6:39], "And he spoke a parable unto them, Can the blind lead the blind? Shall they not both fall into the ditch"?** This is interesting, as parables were spoken to make it possible for even the simplest of people to understand, however even at that, further explanation was sometimes needed to make the required point clear. Some things have not changed. You would think that people in leadership positions could understand this simplicity, and take the appropriate measures to alleviate the very real present and future problems that arise as a result of their "Biblical, psychological and spiritual blindness".

I have to question the mentality of leaders, the questionable "higher powers" that do not have the wherewithal to grasp this simple truth and the mentality of a people who would entrust such incompetents to these influential and authoritative positions. They conduct themselves as though they have been released from their national leadership responsibilities by God himself through their imposition of the "separation of church and state" non-sense. This, however, is of no concern to those proud individuals who, in their self importance and erroneous mentalities, have already excommunicated God from their thinking and thoughts. At least this is what they are using for an excuse to hide behind when matters of a spiritual nature are on the table of which they are totally unprepared to understand and handle.

This exclusion of Biblical orientated mentalities from both leadership, and general populace alike is, like it or not, the real enemy of America, "the enemy within". An individual, a marriage, a family, an organization, a whatever, including a nation, is affected by the leadership, and characterized by the prevailing authority, whether real or false, right or wrong that is in control at the time. The government of a nation assumes essentially the same function as the heart and mind of an individual. If that heart and mind ceases to function properly, the whole body or nation suffers. **[Proverbs 29:2], "When the righteous are in authority, the people rejoice: but when the** wicked beareth rule, the people mourn." [Psalms 127: 1], "Except the Lord build the house, they labor in vain that build it: except the Lord keep the city, the watchman waketh but in vain".

Our nation today, because of her iniquity is in a perpetual state of mourning: it is overrun with its own wickedness, **[Deuteronomy 28:15], "But it shall come to pass, that if thou wilt not hearken unto the voice of the Lord thy God, to observe to do all his commandments and his statutes which I command thee this day; that *all these curses shall come upon thee and overtake thee.*"** Though originally given to the nation of Israel for counsel and direction, the principle applies as much to any nation today as it did to Israel then.

Every day, it seems anymore, there is on the news another account of somewhere in our nation, of a young girl or girls, two this morning [5/9/05]; and that was 3 ½ years ago since I first wrote this paper, it is today, 03/08/08; several since then up to the final revision of this writing, have been violated and found dead. This, in America, the land of the free, and the home of the brave! I could, without much difficulty, find additional and optional adjectives to insert here that would be much more descriptive of America's present condition, all of which would fit quite accurately in our "democratic" nation. If we are determined to impose democracy on the rest of the world, we need to clean it up here first in order to prove to the rest of the world that it is worth having.

It is an everyday occurrence to the shame of America and is not limited to girls. **[1 Peter 5:8], "Be sober, be vigilant; because your adversary the devil, as a roaring lion, walketh about, seeking whom he may devour." [John 10:10], "The thief cometh not, but for to steal, and to kill, and to destroy",** and this adversary devil, this thief, is not particular about his victims. I have said it before and will say it again, "the right of one little girl to live a good life and develop into the person God intended her to be, is greater than all the rights of the people that would prevent this from occurring, including the pornography industry to produce the trash that encourages this abomination.

And the thief continues, with the assistance of his willing henchmen to steal, kill, and destroy the proper God intended function of some, who then set about to do, his evil, dirty work among us. So we are having young people shooting up their schools, killing other students, parents killing their children, children killing parents, and the atrocities go on and on: rape, riot, and murder, rebellion of every type, kind, and description, against God, his word, and the decency of humanity continually. And all this in a democracy, the greatest nation on earth! There is something terribly wrong with this picture.

As long as we remain blind to this, the longer we will continue to suffer as a result, and the worse it will become. **[Hosea 4: 6-7], "My people are destroyed for lack of knowledge: because thou hast rejected knowledge, I will also reject thee, that thou shalt be no priest to me: seeing thou hast forgotten the law "Word" of thy God, I will also forget thy children. As they were increased, so they sinned against me: therefore will I change their glory into shame".**

[Job 4:19-20], "They, who dwell in houses of clay, are destroyed from morning to evening: and perish for ever without any regarding it," and without the sense or intelligence to do so. This is going on continually, day after day in our America; drugs, alcohol, pornography, abortion, etc, destroying our citizens by the multitudes, and yet one 9-11 event and the nation is outraged against a foreign terrorist group who destroys thousands, while our own self imposed internal corruption is destroying millions, **"without any regarding it"**.

America is indeed ripe for God's judgment, and it should be no surprise when it comes, but will neither be acknowledged nor recognized by the vast majority when it does come. Sin does carry with it its own retribution; however, the retribution that America is experiencing in our present time does not seem to be sufficient to compel us to embrace God's solutions to our dilemmas. Maybe if God were to add his judgment to sins own retribution, we might, that is, we might, wake up; but then again we might not. We haven't yet. That could, however, depend on the severity of his judgment.

Considering the rebellious stupidity of mans sin and abominations, I would expect God's judgments to be quite severe. It is amazing how deep stupidity can be in the hearts of men. **[Revelation 9:15-21], vs. 18, "By these three was the third part of men killed, by the fire, and by the smoke, and by the brimstone, which issued out of their mouths. Vs. 20, And the rest of the men which were not killed by these plagues** *yet repented not of the works of their hands*, **that they should not worship devils, and idols of gold, and silver, and brass, and stone, and of wood: which neither can see, nor hear, nor walk: vs.21,** *Neither repented they of their murders, nor of their sorceries, nor of their fornication, nor of their thefts."* When you consider the third part of men, or humanity, being killed by these judgments, it makes 4-5 thousand on 9/11 look like small potatoes, **and still those left alive "repented not".**

Yes indeed, the genetics of stupidity run silent and deep, yet manifested world and nation wide, and not regarded in the soul of man. Neither do they take these things to heart to repent of their pernicious ways, but attempt to silence the truth of the gospel in order to escape the pain of conviction for their multitudes of abominations that the truth constantly reminds them of, **[Acts 7: 51-60].** I realize that there are multitudes of people that will refuse to believe the Biblical accounts of the woes, plagues, punishments, etc; but if they could simply concede to the possibility of them being as recorded, it would seem that the intelligent thing to do would to take measures to escape such horrors. Then if they never happened, you've lost nothing, but if they do occur and you haven't prepared for such an eventuality, you've lost everything for all eternity. Regardless of which way it goes, in the interim, by invoking God's principles in your lifestyle, you will have managed to live a fairly decent lifestyle rather than simply wallowing in a hopeless worldly type existence.

Do you really think you are intelligent enough to oppose God on this and win? I wouldn't count on it, one wrong choice on this one and you are done for eternity. **[Deuteronomy 30:19], "I call heaven and earth to record this day against you, that I have set before you life and death, blessing and cursing, therefore choose life, that both thou and thy seed [descendents] may live."** The lives and eternities of your children in all their tomorrows may well depend on the choice you make today; tomorrow may be too late. Do you love them and value them enough to make the correct choice on their behalf? God has given you a choice in verse 19, and then told you how to choose so **"that both thou and thy seed may live". There is really no way he could make it any simpler.** If your children are going to grow up to make wise, intelligent choices and decisions, they must see these things begin in you.

NOTES

VII.   BOONDOGGLES

In light of the Katrina disaster with all the resulting questionable aid related catastrophes that followed, I decided to write about some of the apparent reasons for such problems and just put them under one short title "BOONDOGGLES". Some of the reasons for this are "political correctness, politics, governmental red tape, constitutionalism with its proponents, and plain old incompetence". They all fit quite well under the term "boondoggles", some being more serious than others. There may well be, and probably are others which the readers are welcome to add at their own discretion, but this should suffice for a launching pad for further comments and ideas. It does seem that the private sector, churches, individuals and other non-governmental groups that were not subject to governmental demands, rules, regulations, requirements, etc. that bound the relief efforts up in politics and red tape, were the ones that were to be credited for getting the jobs done. There are, as usual, exceptions, thanks to the military personal who were deployed and worked so diligently to assist the people who were caught in Katrina's wake, the aftermath of which, psychologically, physically, and financially, will remain long after the material portion is rectified. There were undoubtedly others, and I do not mean to minimize their sacrifices and efforts in bringing aid, comfort, and assistance to those in need. May God bless them abundantly in their many endeavors and help.

In the September 24, 2005 issue of the WORLD magazine, Marvin Olasky wrote an article entitled "Dirty Harry Christians" which I enjoyed very much particularly because it rather complemented some thoughts that I have been rolling around in my mind recently. It seems to boil down to the fact that the well-being of the nation and needs of the people must by all means trump the obstacles raised by the imposition of erroneously applied constitutionalism as demanded by supporters of those things that hinder the establishment and advancement of such well-being. Why should the observance of political and constitutional correctness, as defined by questionable entities, be adhered to when the departure from such will aid and assist those who are in trouble, need help, and save lives? I cannot understand why man, who is supposed to be an intelligent being, imposes all these rules, regulations, stuff and nonsense, when the setting of it aside for a period of time in times of crises would be of great assistance in solving the problems that the crisis causes. Instead they magnify the problems and create additional ones by the imposition of such idiocy at the most inopportune times.

The blending together by the churches and other private agencies, who were not bound by, nor give a rip about political or constitutional red tape, and whatever willing governmental sources that were available and participated, accomplished a great deal in their unity of operation. This was Christianity and good old fashioned Americanism at its best, blended together and united in purpose for the good and well-being of all. Many were well blest and I'm sure God was well pleased with this unity of togetherness. It is too bad it takes such tragedy to bring people together, united in common purpose for the good of all. This is exactly what God has been trying to get people to do for centuries, united together according to his will, design, and purpose for the well-being of his entire creation, but just like people being warned of the impending doom of Katrina, the majority have not, do not; and will not, heed the warnings. And just like the aftermath of Katrina, God will get the blame for it. It is amazing how the multitudes have no thought or regard of God until something disastrous occurs for which they feel justified in blaming him.

Mr. Olasky posed the question, where's the ACLU? Why haven't they stuck their noses into this demanding that the church stay out of the government's business of meeting the needs required? Do you suppose these little ducks found themselves in a puddle of muck much to large for them to negotiate and as a result decided to keep their incessant quacking quiet? Maybe they drummed up enough intelligence among the whole lot of them to realize that the government was not up to the task considering the magnitude of the situation, and they themselves certainly could offer no assistance with the problems faced. However to offer solutions to problems would be way out of their normal function of causing problems rather than solving them, but then intelligence is not required to cause them. It does take a considerable amount of it, however, to solve them.

Maybe that's why humanity in general is more proficient in causing problems rather than finding solutions and solving them. Solving problems would require something of humanity that their evil nature does not provide: however, enter, God. We have two options here, to listen to man in his idiocy and continue downward in our demise, or listen to God in his wisdom and see if we can dig up enough intelligence and courage to implement it to the solving of our multiplying dilemma's. In view of what man has done to his world through his pride, arrogance, ignorance, and stupidity, it would be the intelligent thing to opt for God and his righteous counsel. If the ACLU wishes to argue the point to defend their position of nothingness, they may do so providing they can find some one willing to waste their time to listen to them with their empty, pointless rhetoric that leads nowhere, provides nothing of constructive, positive nature, and leaves the soul in poverty, **[3 John: 2], "Beloved, I wish above all things that thou mayest prosper and be in health, even as thy soul prospereth"**. As for me and my house, we will serve the Lord. I have heard the

ACLU people talk; they present nothing of substance, and they add nothing to me and certainly nothing to the nation. But then we have some factions in government that seem to have those same characteristics.

Now concerning God and his Word of Truth and Absolutes: **[Psalms 111:10; 119:104],[Proverbs 1:7; 4:5; 4:7; 9:10]**. There is an interesting second half to **Proverbs 1:7** following the exhortation to fear, or reverence God for the beginning of knowledge, it continues; **"but fools despise wisdom and instruction"**. Here is an apt description of those who oppose God and his counsel of righteousness. We find contained in this selection of scriptures the very basic necessities for a successful life. Of course these things from a Biblical position cannot be attained to outside of God. It is apparent, from the present condition of our world, that man has failed miserably in his attempt to operate and manage this world on his own without these that are available only within God obtained requirements and necessities.

The ACLU and like organizations with their sympathizers and proponents squawk and spew forth their ridiculous nonsense, but when the chips are down and solutions are needed and people need help, they are quite silent and nowhere to be found. They remind me of a quotation from Shakespeare, **"Tis as a tale told by an idiot, full of sound and fury, signifying nothing"**. Well said William, I hope you don't mind my borrowing some of your material from time to time; it fits as well in today's society; as it did in yours; maybe even more so, I dare say, as there are more idiots for it to apply to and they've invented devious new and improved ways to be idiots, as **"inventors of evil things"**, **[Romans 1:30]**.

There is a possibility however, as the television commercial says, "we didn't invent them, we just improved, or should we say, developed them". **[Hosea 4: 6-7],"My people are destroyed for lack of knowledge, [willful ignorance], [without even sufficient knowledge to know it is ignorance]: because thou hast rejected knowledge, I will also reject thee that thou shalt be no priest to me: seeing thou hast forgotten the law of thy God, I will also forget thy children. As they were increased, so they sinned against me: therefore I will change their glory into shame"**. Certainly America is experiencing the increase in population and we see signs everyday of the increase of sin with its intensity and viciousness throughout our beloved, nation. We have seen America in her days of glory; are we now on the brink of suffering shame at least to the same extent as we enjoyed our glory because of our "boondoggles" in serving God, thus is *"iniquity found in thee"*.

Indeed, we are witnessing a horrible increase in abominations, and their results, on a daily basis in our nation as graphic testimony to this increase and intensity. And still man maintains his rebellion and ignorance: ignorance of God, his thinking and ways, ignorance of the things man needs to avoid, and ignorance of the method, the only method available, he is to employ in doing so. This whole process will require and elevate a person to level of intense study and exploration of God's word that this world knows nothing about and continues to despise, **[Isaiah 5: 24], "Therefore as the fire devoureth the stubble, and the flame consumeth the chaff, so their root shall be as rottenness, and their blossom shall go up as dust: because they have cast away the law of the Lord of hosts, and despised the word of the Holy One of Israel"**. This has certainly become *"the way of the world"*.

[Romans 12: 2], "Be not conformed to this world: but be ye transformed by the renewing of your mind, that you may prove what is that good, and acceptable, and perfect will of God". However, the intense study required for this may be the very reason and excuse he uses to avoid it, [**Ecclesiastes 12: 12**], **"And further, by these my son, be admonished: of making many books there is no end;** ***and much study is a weariness of the flesh"***. It is this "weariness of the flesh" in pursuit of Godly attainments that man has a propensity to avoid, thus remaining ignorant and "without the essential knowledge" that would avert his destruction. Consequently, [**Job 4: 20-21**], **"They are destroyed from morning to evening: they perish forever without any regarding it. Doth not their excellency which is in them go away? They die, even without wisdom"**. Consider this: sin is not our problem; it is stupidity; the lack of wisdom with its implementation of knowledge that would cause us to refrain from indulgence in sin: that is the problem, [**Hosea 4: 6**]. It is imperative that we **"get a vision of the value"** of this Godly counsel of the excellency and essential knowledge that prevents us from the stupidity of indulgence in sin and iniquity resulting in error and destruction.

Mr. Olasky's reference and use of "Dirty Harry" in his article was very appropriate concerning the Christians involved in the Katrina aftermath. Dirty Harry didn't have any use for the binding rules, regulations, restrictions, laws, etc. that, in effect, bound him up in red tape, obstructed justice and prevented the solutions needed to solve the problems. It does sound terribly like some of the "boondoggles" that we have heard about and are still hearing about in Katrina's aftermath. A friend of mine and I used to discuss things such as this when we were working together. We talked of the pessimist, the optimist, and then we decided we would add a third; a peptimist. As usual, the pessimist said it couldn't be done, the optimist said it could be done, and while they were busy having dialogue and discussion over the possibilities concerning it, the peptimist was busy doing it and getting it done. God bless the Christian "peptimists" and anyone else who didn't allow the "red tape" to hinder nor prevent them from doing what needed to be done for whoever needed it, regardless of race, color or creed.

That, world, that, ACLU, is Christianity with it's principles in action without "separation of church and state" or in spite of it and its proponents and supporters, including the ACLU. As the Church of Jesus Christ of **[Matthew 16:18]** as provided through Almighty God himself by his word is the sole owner and supplier of the principles, values, and standards that have formed the foundation upon which America was built, God alone has the right, wisdom, understanding, knowledge and intelligence to manage this world and this nation. This blubbering opposition that comes in from the sidelines is disgusting to say the least regardless of who it is, or where it comes from. It is inappropriate, out of place, and is tending to the destruction of this great nation, and as the destroyer, has no rights whatsoever. **"The thief cometh not but to steal, to kill, and to destroy", [John 10: 10]** and those that oppose the **"righteousness that exalteth a nation" are part of the thief's crowd that condones the sin that is a reproach to any people, [Proverbs 14: 34]. [Deuteronomy 30: 19]:** By their choosing **"death and cursing"** instead of **"life and blessing"** as their lifestyle, they are directly tending to, and strongly contributing to America's demise and destruction.

Wake up America; the thief and his cohorts are inside your tent, NOW. He, she, they, them, whoever, whatever, that is opposed to the establishing and proclamation of the **"gospel of deliverance and peace"** as is presented in the word of the "God of peace" *are enemies* of that peace and the deliverance, tranquility, and strength that it provides for the people and nation that embrace and practice it. The principle found in **[Deuteronomy 4: 5-9]** certainly is applicable and desperately needed, even in our New Testament times. Unfortunately it is neither recognized nor considered. *Somehow rights have* *replaced treason when the idea of treason should prevail, however treason has been reduced to simply "freedom of expression"; another victim of "relativity".*

How in the world did such trash ever get a foothold and anchored in our American mentality? Is it possible that the American mentality has become so insidiously polluted with iniquitous, worldly leaven of trash and garbage that it can no longer even recognize the dangers it has allowed by its anti-Bible, anti-God idiocy that has become the norm for its thinking and behavior? Who is responsible for its insidious introduction and establishment? I am afraid the **blind leading the blind** principle has wider and deeper implications pertaining to stupidity and destruction than we ever realized. Some had to introduce this while others stood by and allowed it to happen. Where were the "watchdogs" that failed to sound the alarm? Do we even have anyone with the spiritual and mental depth perception needed to recognize the dangers, and sound the alarm or the wisdom and intelligence to take appropriate measures to deal with it?

The blinded to the truth, contrary minded henchmen of the thief and destroyer are to be found among us, as the apostle Paul put it, **"mine own countrymen"**, **[2 Corinthians 11:26]-[1 Thessalonians 2:14]**. It makes no difference as to their citizenship, it is the concepts, the beliefs, the ideologies, and attitudes of mind that determine the loyalty, allegiance, and commitment of a person, whether or not they are Americans who claim to be committed to the things that strengthen and preserve a people and nation that are provided and taught by the righteous counsel of God, **[Psalms 1:1-3]**. For instance: a Muslim may be an American citizen, live among us, work among us, etc, but their loyalty and allegiance is still to Islam, the Koran, and it's teachings which are contrary to the Biblical principles on which America was established and founded, consequently, they are contrary to America, its Christian belief's and Americanism. Only utter stupidity would allow this to continue. Tolerance and diversity in this area is not only anti-American, its anti-Bible, **[Isaiah 26: 8-10], "Yea, in the way of thy judgments, O Lord, have we waited for thee; the desire of our soul is to thy name, and to the remembrance of thee. With my soul have I desired thee in the night; yea, with my spirit within me will I seek thee early;** *for when thy judgments are in the earth, the inhabitants of the world will learn righteousness,* [but not until then]. *Let favor,* [tolerance and diversity, etc,] *be showed to the wicked, yet he will not learn righteousness; in the land of uprightness will he deal unjustly, and will not behold the majesty of the Lord.*

[Revelation 21: 27] gives us essential insight as to how God will deal with this sort of situation to keep it from becoming a problem. Deal with it God's way and the righteous don't have a problem, only the transgressors of righteousness have the problem. Not dealing with it God's way, and even the righteous have problems they can't handle nor solve, for they will only be alleviated by God's method's of dealing with them.

I can't help but be amused when I hear people say concerning a certain situation or set of circumstances; "Oh, he or she is just trying to play God". I cannot help but think, how refreshing, in a world filled with iniquity and sin where the vast majority are playing the devil's part; that someone has the courage and intestinal fortitude to stand up amongst all the trash, garbage, stupidity, and contrariness man has heaped upon himself and take God's side and play his part. How wonderfully refreshing this would be! I see this as an attempt at some sort of underhanded accusation of belittlement, as though there is something wrong with this action, when we were indeed created in God's image and likeness I would accept it as a compliment instead.

Again, how wonderfully refreshing this would be! Indeed, are not all born again, professing Christians supposed to be living in a manner that exemplifies this, **[Acts 17: 28], "For in him we live and move and have our being; as certain also of your own poets have said, For we are also his offspring".** **[Genesis 1: 26], "And God said, *let us make man in our image, after our likeness:* and let them have dominion over the fish of the sea, and over the fowl of the air, and over the cattle, and over all the earth, and over every creeping thing that creepeth upon the earth".**

A constitution that was designed to provide for the wellbeing of a nation, but is twisted around to allow destructive elements to foment and develop within that nation and tends to its demise and ultimate destruction is less than worthless. In addition, those who are responsible for this atrocity of a twisted constitution, are equally as worthless and disqualify themselves as leaders and authorities of the nation they represent. Cast aside and reject the principles that are the strength and stability of a nation, and you immediately identify yourself as an enemy of that nation and people, thus your professed loyalty and allegiance goes in favor of the thief. Of such is the subtlety and deception of the "thief". Thus the "blind" are committed to following the "blind" with both headed for the ditch of destruction and dragging those under their evil influence along with them, including eventually, the entire nation: and all that was done in the past to make that nation great is in vain. **[Psalms 127: 1], "Except the Lord build the house, they labor in vain that build it; except the Lord keep the city, the watchman waketh but in vain".**

It is a good thing and a proper thing to provide assistance to the physical and material needs of the oppressed and destitute, but in the final culmination of all things, it is nothing but a band-aid effort if provision for the preservation of their eternal souls is not met. This is the ultimate of importance. It is good and necessary to provide this assistance to the needy, but the greatest "boondoggle" and tragedy of all is **"to leave the weightier matters of the law, judgment, justice, and mercy, the presenting of the gospel of salvation through Jesus Christ, "undone", [Matthew 23: 23]-[Luke 11: 42]. [John 3: 1-12] presents a truth that the world refuses and will not accept, "Ye must be born again".** The rulers of the Jews, verse 1, and the masters of Israel, verse 10, did not know or accept this truth; so it is with the rulers and masters of America as well as the wannabe's. *Until there is a change in the prevailing thinking and the prevailing ways as a result of such change of thinking and thought, this once great nation will continue in its downward spiral, annihilating herself by her own erroneous mindset of opposition to God.*

Though the spiritual leaders of a nation, who by the way need to be busy about upgrading their own competence in Biblical truth, spiritual matters, and responsibilities, to supply spiritual leadership and guidance for the people and nation: this does not release the civil leaders from their God mandated responsibilities of assisting and encouraging these spiritual leaders in the proclamation of God's word and this gospel of Jesus Christ in all it's truth, absolutes, and accuracy. The ruling entities of a nation were never intended to be formed and operated outside God's counsel of righteousness, but be subject to these principles, the actual "higher powers", for guidance and direction as part of the church. Because of transgression of this, disunity between these two entities, civil and spiritual leaders, plus the warfare that rages within each as a result of their own mental poverty of erroneous thought concerning spiritual matters and responsibilities, is the reason for all the problems we are experiencing today in our society, nation, and the world.

Then, of course, we have the initiators and instigators of dissension and division among us of "our own countrymen" who care not for the people or nation and its well-being according to God's ways, but are only committed to their own self interest agendas which in the end will prove only to be disastrous in their concepts, operations, and results. It is a sad commentary on America when the populace begins to think that America is great because she teaches and embraces such things as, diversity without necessary discrimination, and discrimination without wisdom, understanding, knowledge, and intelligence for guidance and discretion. America is also experiencing tolerance and acceptance without wisdom and understanding of the erroneous consequences of the misapplication of these things. There is endless dialogue, debating, and discourse over a multitude of issues, most without value or substance, and continually engaged in without any **"knowledge of the holy" [Proverbs 9:10; 30:3].**

[Job 38: 1-3], "Then the Lord answered Job out of a whirlwind, and said, Who is this that darkeneth counsel by words without knowledge. Gird up now thy loins [America] like a man: for I will demand of thee, and answer thou me". All this indiscriminating diversity, tolerance and acceptance of practices, and conduct contrary to the foundational structure and maintenance of a strong nation based on Godly principles, has to be considered as sin and the ultimate foolishness and absolute stupidity. This is, however, the condition of man without God. **[Proverbs 14: 34], "Righteousness exalteth a nation: but sin is a reproach on any people".** America is not exempt from this. We have brought a reproach on ourselves because of no correction of the shame we have created and burdened ourselves with because of, **"the iniquity that is found in thee", [Ezekiel 28; 15].**

It seems that America, even in the midst of her internal problems, in trying to maintain itself as a viable entity, has wrapped itself in a worn, tattered, shredded, blanket of boondoggles, the greatest of which and from which all the others proceed, is **the casting away of the law, principles, of the Lord of hosts, and despising the Word of the Holy One of Israel, in short, the rebellion against, and rejection of God, [Isaiah 5: 24].** As for Israel, God is not finished with her, but as his chosen people will, **[Genesis 12:2-3], "bless them that bless thee and curse him that curseth thee: and in thee shall all the families of the earth be blessed".** God is still the God of Abraham, Isaac, and Jacob, and the Holy One of Israel, and he is not blind to those who curse her, nor is he blind to Israel's transgressions which he will deal with in his own way as he always has in the past. However God deals with the situation, it is his business; we will do well to take care of our own. He is the God of righteousness and the God of those who specialize in righteousness and holiness, **[Acts 10:35],** and his name is Jehovah; [Yahweh in Hebrew].

There are those individuals, organizations, and groups within the borders of our great nation who conduct themselves as true American's, manifesting Christian characteristics and attitudes, both within our country and countries around the world in support of the oppressed, both physically and spiritually. The basic hindrances to their noble endeavors are the attitudes and actions of oppressive governments and the contrary ideologies within and protected by those governmental structures, many of which are founded on contrary religious beliefs. There has been just recently within our nation, a phrase come to the surface of realism called "culture of corruption". I do not know who first coined it, but I can certainly understand the prompting behind it as it fits the vast majority of the cultures of our chaotic world including our own America. Thank God, there is a **"Ye must be born again Christian culture alive and well among us"** that is providing a little strength and stability for the nation. They may be a minority in quantity, but definitely a majority in quality.

Before I conclude this article on **"Boondoggles"**, there are a couple other scripture's found in **[Deuteronomy 10: 12-13]** that I would like to leave with you for your consideration, both for leaders and followers alike. **Consider removing the name "Israel" and replacing it with "America" or possibly with your own name.** This may give you a whole new understanding of the content of the Old Testament and possibly of the whole Bible. **"And now Israel, "America, your name", what doth the Lord thy God require of thee, but to fear the Lord thy God, to walk in all his ways, and to love him, and to serve the Lord thy God with all thy heart and with all thy soul, To keep the commandments of the Lord, and his statutes, which I command thee this day <u>FOR THY GOOD"</u>**. It is my sincere hope and prayer that this writing will help you to "weed out" the personal "boondoggles" of your own life, displacing and replacing them with the whole counsel of God.

NOTES

NOTES

IX. PANDEMIC

Pandemic: a rather sinister sounding word to say the least, with the potential to cause pandemonium among those not prepared for such disasters. It is not normally used and probably unfamiliar to most of us, but nevertheless used quite extensively recently in relation to something referred to as the bird flu. This is all quite new to me as I had never heard of the bird flu and don't really recall the use of the word "pandemic". I was quite taken by the concern that was expressed over the potential danger that seems possible, not proven, if in fact there were to be a world-wide outbreak of this bird flu thing. I really don't know what all the concern is, considering man has by his own hand, and proven I might add, killed, slaughtered, annihilated, destroyed etc., millions over the centuries by a pandemic that could be referred to, but not normally spoken of, as **"sin", "the wages of which continue to be death"**. This might offend some with sensitive ears not normally used to facing the truth of this destructive element that is alive and well among us and being promoted with increasing gusto. [Hosea 4: 7], **"As they were increased, so they sinned against me: therefore will I change their glory into shame"**.

Because there is pleasure and financial profit in sin, among various other reasons, man embraces, pursues, and practices it continually. By it **[Job 4:20], "They are destroyed from morning to evening: they perish forever without any regarding it"**, and will fight to defend their right to thus destroy themselves in their pursuit of these death dealing practices and pleasures. I take no delight in having to identify with these miserable humanistic specimens of ignorance, as I live among them, look something like many of them, walk and move about as they do, and at one time was one of them, indulging myself in the same stupidity, **[Ephesians 2: 1-3]**. And if it were not for the amazing grace of God, I would very probably still be conducting myself among them even as they continue to destroy themselves. **"But God, verses 4-10, who is rich in mercy, for his great love wherewith he loved, and continues to love, us", sent his Son Jesus Christ to rescue me, redeem me, wash away my sin, and reconcile me back to himself to live and move and have my being in him and experience great, perfect peace, fullness of joy unspeakable and full of glory at his right hand where there are pleasures for evermore. [John 3: 16; Acts 17: 28; Isaiah 26: 3; 1 Peter 1: 8; Psalms 16: 11].**

This eternal provision of God is available to whosoever will avail themselves of it. **That is what awaits those who chose to go through the strait gate and walk the narrow way that leads to life everlasting in the presence of the Lord. On the other hand there is the broad gate and the wide road of sinful pandemic that multiplied millions have chosen to remain on that leads to eternal death, misery, and destruction; [Matthew 7: 13-14].** Enjoying the sinful pursuits that are characteristic of this road to death is certainly no intelligent reason for remaining there **and rejecting God's invitation to life and blessing versus death and cursing, [Deuteronomy 30:19], "For the wages of sin is still death, but the gift of God is still eternal life, [Romans 6: 23].** These truths and Biblical principles have not changed over the centuries since God established them nor will they ever change, **[Matthew 24:35; Mark 13:31; Luke 21:33].**

Pandemics may come, and pandemics may go, **but God's word and those that walk therein shall go on forever, [Matthew 24: 35; Mark 13: 31; Luke21:33].** Pandemics; tsunamis, hurricanes, volcanoes, earthquakes, floods, tornadoes, storms of ever type, kind, and intensity; famines, pestilences, plagues, and sin in its beginning through its advanced stages indulged in its multitude of various forms and practices at mans discretion and evil choices, take your pick. Some have been experienced, and many are being experienced yet today. Many are yet to be experienced, but when the winds of opposition have stopped blowing and the dust of ignorance and rebellion have settled, standing as tall, strong and as victorious as ever will be God's word and those who have trusted in him and embraced that word as life itself, for indeed it is.

It is amazing how that man has created his own pandemic of destruction by rebellion against God, which not only destroys the body but also destroys the soul in hell; plus destroying everything else it touches. Then as man witnesses the judgment of God taking place on this iniquity and abomination, he neither realizes what is taking place, nor does he have the wherewithal to admit that he has brought it on himself. **[Jeremiah 12:10-11], "Many pastors, civil rulers, have destroyed my vineyards, they have trodden my portion underfoot, they have made my pleasant portion a desolate wilderness. They have made it desolate, and being desolate it mourneth unto me; the whole land is made desolate, BECAUSE NO MAN LAYETH IT TO HEART", [Romans 8: 19-23].** Ask yourself this question; could this be referring to a spiritual, mental, psychological, desolation, which ultimately results in all manner of other desolation?

The prospects of the answers are quite interesting and thought provoking, eliciting at the very least, and possibily, some informative educational discussion, dialogue, and plain old fashioned study that could well result in **the knowledge needed to prevent the destruction of people, adults and children, including you and yours; [Hosea 4:6].** You will have to admit; it's rather an interesting subject; and because **"you and yours" are involved whether you like it or not,** making it worthy of intelligent and diligent study, and pursuit. Try it: you just might learn to like it. At any rate, the exercising of your mind will do you, and it, some good.

Unfortunately, concerning the "Christian Religion", spiritually speaking, America is generally suffering from a "brain dead" pandemic, with of course the exception of the "few" exceptions that are on the **narrow way of [Matthew 7:14]. The rest, the many, are on the broad road of eternal pandemic destruction that will make the "bird flu" at its worst as well as the 9/11 event seem like a Sunday School picnic.** This is not intended to frighten people, nor to anger, or even to offend them, however if it provides enough shock treatment to awaken a few to realize that all this might be worth some investigation, at least they will be started in the right direction. Let me assure you, whatever you do to escape that "eternal pandemic destruction" will be well worth whatever it takes including the time and effort spent in doing so, including bringing unity back into the church. Your eternity is definitely worth at least giving it some serious, intelligent, thought and consideration. Don't victimize yourself by closing your mind to the possibilities that are available through the exploration and discoveries that await you in Biblical truth and studies.

The blind lead the blind, both headed for the "pandemic" ditch of destruction. If you are a blind follower, awaken to the fact you needn't remain a blind follower, but become a wide awake leader walking in the light of God's word and bringing that word of deliverance to many of your past acquaintances, even the blind leaders. There is no limit to the possibilities and potential that are available through Jesus Christ, the God provided Saviour and Redeemer of mankind, who, **[2 Peter 1:3-4] "According as his divine power hath given unto us all things that pertain unto life and Godliness, through the knowledge of him that hath called us to glory and virtue, Whereby are given unto us exceeding great and precious promises: that by these ye might** be partakers of the divine nature, having escaped the corruption that is in the world through lust".

There is an ingredient of sin that may well be a foundational cause of sin itself that we should take a good look at as it manifests itself at times very naturally when our attention is diverted from being **"sober and vigilant", [1 Peter 5: 8].** This **"pandemic of selfishness"** has wreaked havoc among mankind since his beginning, but the world doesn't seem to be concerned about it or the devastation it causes, or making any attempt at correcting it, but to the contrary, spend lifetimes embracing it. This, however, is understandable as the only certain measure of correction is found within God and his Word of Truth, the gospel of Jesus Christ. Because the world is blind to sin it naturally would be blind to its causes, becoming irritated from time to time with selfishness and the way it adversely affects them, but never acquainting it with the sin in their own lives. It's always something that is present and operative in someone else's life, but it's something that will never happen to me, or at least in a way that it can't somehow be deviously justified, at least to my own satisfaction.

Yes, I am a born-again Christian, but I have a pretty good knowledge of the way the world thinks in their efforts to vindicate themselves of any wrong doing. After all, Adam said it was the woman's fault, the woman said it was the serpents fault, and thus the principle of man's invention of "passing the buck" was begun. The serpent had no one to blame but the blame was not all his, he provided the opportunity to rebel but Adam and Eve did the rebelling. God did not ask; Adam what did Eve cause you to do, nor to Eve, what did the serpent cause you to do, but direct questions, **"Hast THOU eaten of the tree, whereof I commanded thee that THOU shouldest not eat? [Genesis 3: 11-13]. To Eve, "What is this THOU HAST DONE?** All three of them were to bear their own result of transgression, and we are all still paying for it and still trying to **"pass the buck". "The devil made me do it", "Well if God is a God of love, I just don't understand how he could have allowed this to happen", "It's an act of God", and the indignant idiocy continues on, unabated and still without "knowledge" as man still attempts to absolve himself of the guilt of his abominable transgressions.** And the "pandemic" of stupidity continues to roll downward toward hell and pick up bulk and speed as it goes, and from within the mass you can hear, "it's his fault, it's her fault, it's their fault, it's the Democrats fault, it's the Republicans fault".

Everyone knows someone on who to fix the blame, but no one knows how to fix the problems, and if they don't get fixed, there's always someone we can blame for that, and we can always find justifiable reasons for doing just that. And the "pandemic" of stupidity continues, in the church, in the state, in the populace, in the nation; wherever you find people you will find an abundance of the "pandemic" as man continues to destroy himself in rebellion against God, choosing death and cursing in preference to life and blessing and blaming someone else for the results. You will have to agree, that constitutes a "pandemic of stupidity and ignorance". Are you being destroyed by it, or feeling the effects of someone you love being destroyed by it?

The bird flu may kill many if it materializes, but while we wait to see if it does, we are already in the process of destroying thousands among us by our own **"lack of the knowledge" that would prevent such destruction.** The means to such an end are available to all: **[Deuteronomy 30:14; Romans 10: 8-10], "The word is nigh thee, even in thy mouth, and in thy heart: that is, the word of faith, which we preach; That if thou shalt confess with thy mouth the Lord Jesus, and shalt believe in thine heart that God hath raised him from the dead, thou shalt be saved. For with the heart man believeth unto righteousness;**

and with the mouth confession is made unto salvation". [John 3:16-17], **"For God so loved the world, that he gave his only begotten Son, that whosoever believeth on him should not perish, but have everlasting life". For God sent not his Son into the world to condemn the world; but that the world through him might be saved".** The God provided means to a God ordained glorious eternal provision are available to all men every where so that they are without excuse. Their transgressions and the terrible results are upon their own heads and the "buck passing" is over.

NOTES

VII.   LIFE

Life, I believe it is safe to say that most, if not all of us, were propelled into it without our permission. Had we known what we were getting into and had a choice we may well have declined the opportunity to participate. Looking back on my own life, I have to admit, I have nothing to complain about and am very thankful for my 74 years of time on this earth. Had I exercised some wisdom which I knew nothing about, I could have made things much better, but I thank God for his hand of protection and unbeknown to me at the time, a whole lot of wonderful deliverance. There are some things that I would change if I had it to do over again, but I suppose we could all say that.

However, what is past is past, never to be recaptured and we realize all we have left is a future and whatever we make of it. That reality usually comes along sometime after we become aware of the fact we have already made a mess out of a good portion of life, which only now becomes a part of the past with little or nothing we can do to correct it. Had I not started out so young and ignorant I may have done better at many things, however as I got older, the condition of young was lost somewhere in the dust of the past, however, I begin to realize that this ignorance thing stuck with me and had picked up a companion called stupidity which also plagued me from time to time, and at times quite often. All of this seemed to be built on a platform of "dumb", all of which many years later I learned through some rather extensive Bible study was covered under what the Bible termed in **[Hosea 4:6] as a "lack of knowledge", which in a word was "ignorance". I was to realize that through "much study which is a weariness to the flesh", [Ecclesiastes 12: 12],** that the gaining of knowledge, thus a cure for ignorance was somewhat available. However, to continue in a position of refusal to avail oneself of the availability of such knowledge is plain stupid, which I found was much more difficult to cure.

Ignorance isn't that bad if applied to specific things that require specialized training and study to familiarize oneself of them but have no need for. **But,** to willingly choose to remain ignorant of the necessities that every day life and life more abundantly consist of is not good, and it gets worse as the stupidity continues and intensifies, which it has a nasty habit of doing. That is the way sin works; if not dealt with according to God's method of deliverance it becomes like a snowball rolling down hill, it builds and grows in mass, bulk, and speed until something big enough and strong enough can bring it to a halt. Enter God's program of deliverance, redemption, and reconciliation through Jesus Christ, God's once for all time, for everyone's, sacrifice for all sin. To willing remain ignorant of these "essential things" that pertain to enrichment of life as God intended we should have and enjoy, when they are so available and encouraged by the very need of them, is to manifest extreme stupidity and idiocy, **[Proverbs 1:7], "The fear of the Lord is the beginning of wisdom: but fools despise wisdom and instruction"**.

Unfortunately it took a lot of years and experiences, many of which were unpleasant, before the full realization of all this begin to set in, and now having begin to set in, I still had to learn how to correct the situation. That was the hard part. The simplicity of it amazed me, as it became apparent it was all a matter of making the right choices, which was something I didn't have much experience with. Now all I had to do was figure out what the right choices were. I learned that the wrong choices were many and came quite naturally while the right ones but a few and harder to make than the wrong ones simply because the wrong ones catered to my "feelings". These feelings, which seemed to be prevalent in humanity, were the forerunners of the "if it feels good, do it" philosophy that was to become the societal norm in our American culture and is still pretty much in control of it today.

The wrong choices just seemed so natural while the right ones difficult because they had to be learned and then, in the process of learning them, which was very slow, I had to exercise a thing called "self discipline" to initiate them. This self discipline thing also became a bit of a problem. It was easier to talk and think about than it was to do because my feelings and emotions always got in the way. I found that it was easier to go to school and learn reading, writing, and arithmetic and a few other things they taught in school, and some they didn't, than it was to attain to wisdom, understanding, knowledge and Godly counsel and intelligence and then initiate it. It seems as though this is still a major hang-up with humanity. Even common sense was rather hard to get a grip on. Knowledge: if I studied hard enough, another problem, I could gain vast amounts of knowledge. Obviously I didn't study hard enough so the vastness of knowledge eluded me, but one way or another I did pick up a little of it in various areas along the way. This, I am convinced was another area of God's divine deliverance, guidance and amazing grace. I am sure Mom and Dad's prayers had much to do with this. God is gracious, even to idiots who have a somewhat difficult time of learning, generally by their own choice.

For instance, my dear mother, who I learned later was much smarter than I, had me held over in the first grade because she said I was a poor reader. I was a slow starter. Now that I've been fortunate enough to live to the leading edge of old age I hope to be a slow finisher too. I complained about this first grade holdover later in life by telling Mom that I could read as good as any and better than most. She simply replied; it did you some good then didn't it? It's pretty tough to argue against that sort of logic.

However, with the whole situation approximately sixty-eight years past tense, it doesn't make much difference any more, except my Mother's decision was a wise one which I have benefited from these many years gone by. Thanks Mom for being a whole lot smarter than I realized you were at the time. It seems that the older and smarter I became, the smarter Mom got. Strange indeed, how that works, but I think I'm finally beginning to understanding it. Mother tried to teach me some things later in life that I never realized were as important as they were until many years later, and had I learned them when she was trying to teach them to me I would, without a doubt, be better off because of them today. Anyway, that will always exist as a lost possibility. Who knows, maybe I wouldn't have learned them well enough to take advantage of the situations that presented themselves and to use them profitably with Godly wisdom, knowledge, and understanding for all concerned anyhow.

On the leading edge of old age it doesn't make much difference anymore. But, ve do grow to soon old un to late schmart. I was certainly no exception to this. Here I am older and it seems as though "schmarts" still manage to elude me with considerable regularity. So; in all of this, from being born, to childhood, to teenager, to born again, married to a wonderful lady, three children, all of whom assisted in the continuation of my education: life continued.

Then through an enjoyable electrical career to semi-retirement, then to retirement and a change from electrician to writer which opened up and demanded new knowledge in a new area which I am struggling with but enjoying immensely, I continue on enjoying the opportunities I have been blessed with.

God has blessed me abundantly in spite of my ignorance and moments of stupidity which are not as extensive as they were when I was much younger but still managed to hang around and make themselves known from time to time. Praise be unto God for his patience and longsuffering; things are increasingly looking and becoming better now, in spite of a world that seems to be coming apart at the seams.

The intensity of my youthful born again experience picked up momentum after my short four year naval career and I was married to that wonderful lady, who with God's help was able to intensify that Christian experience, and my education in Christian character building. I became associated with a wonderful pastor friend, Bob Roberts, who was to become one of my closest and dearest friends and contributed greatly to my spiritual growth and development over the years. There were of course others who contributed greatly to this growth and development process over the years since up to the present day. We were blessed with this elderly pastor's presence at our 50th wedding anniversary celebration on Feb. 20th 2005. What a wonderful time we had. If I had it to do over again, I would marry the same lady and have the same children, which is one of the areas of life that has been extremely enjoyable. There have been a few bumps in the road, **"but God, [Ephesians 2: 4], who is rich in mercy, for his great love wherewith he loves us, has kept us secure in that love".** I believe I have finally begun to learn, assess, and appreciate the value of developing and enriching a relationship of intimate fellowship with God and enjoying the blessings of his continual presence. How I wish I had attained to this years ago.

This is just a brief summary of my life from birth to the leading edge of old age which I expect to continue for awhile although one never knows about those things so it is best to be ready to meet God at all times. Here I have just hit the high spots. I don't know if the rest would be all that interesting to others although to some it might be. My life to me was a very interesting one, much of it I would be willing to repeat with certain changes, additions, and certainly, omissions. I do not, however, have any complaints. I have outlived many and with quite good health and with a multitude of God's richest blessings, I hope to continue on yet for awhile. What lies ahead certainly holds more promise than that which is past. I have enjoyed a multitude of dear friends, many from school days whom I have the pleasure of seeing from time to time especially at high school reunions each year. These reunions are kept alive and well by our senior class president Bill Bear and his dear wife Joey. Many thanks to them for their time, energies, and expenses! We have had some great times together with that portion of the class that has in the past, and still responds to their efforts. I may in the future fill in some of the places between the high spots mentioned here. I cannot refer to them as the low spots because there was nothing low about them. They were all high places. As a cousin, Alvin Hagerman, once told me, man, you've got to be the luckiest kid alive. Looking back I believe I was. I just wish I had realized and appreciated it more at the time. Thanks Mom and Dad for a great childhood and life.

There are indeed, by God's grace better times ahead, blest I trust, with increasing wisdom, knowledge, understanding, intelligence, and plain old common sense. All these make for better companions than some of those I spent much of my time with in my earlier years. Consequently some of those those companions never added anything to me, but then I never added much to them either. But such is the ignorance of youth. We did enjoy some good times together, but like most young people probably learned more about things we shouldn't do than we did about things we should do. This became more apparent as the years went by and additional intelligence was accumulated. Thank God for his abundant forgiveness and multiplied blessings as I continue enjoying his presence along life's journey.

There is no doubt in my mind that God's answers to Mom and Dad's prayers kept me delivered and safe from falling into a lot of chuck holes that I created with my stupidity and ignorance on the road of life. There is more to this "growing to soon old un to late schmart" that people need to think, meditate about and come to realize. It never ceases to amaze me that even with the time and energy saving devices that have been introduced and developed over that last 50-70 years we seem to have less time than we ever did. Certainly these devices have allowed us to be involved in a multitude of additional things than we would have had time for previously and we promptly inundated ourselves with a conglomeration of these new and exciting things rather than stepping back and analyzing where a lack of intense thinking and thought concerning these things was taking us.

One day we were to wake up to realize that these things, this stuff, had taken control of our lives and instead of living as God intended and designed us to live with the peace that passes understanding, fullness of joy, realized purpose of being, etc, etc. We were reduced to an existence of feeding some sort of worldly, political machine that dictates to us how we are to proceed and struggle on; all for the sake of governmental designed and directed "political correctness". I have, however, over the past few years, built up a bit of a resistance to these man created things that are causing more problems as the days go by.

It seems that governmental and secular political correctness has become the order of the day for our society and nation. I have, due to a bit of a rebellious streak against being herded into a "corral of compliance" by these ones who have excommunicated God and his Word through the erroneous "separation of church and state" nonsense, decided not to participate in this political correctness. I have on the other hand, decided to exercise and stay with **"Biblical Correctness"**, and invite any and all to join me in the exiting journey of exploration and discovery in the life building treasures found within the confines of God's Word of Truth and Absolutes.

We will all make a few mistakes along the way; but better to make a mistake that can be corrected when heading in the right direction than continuing in the wrong direction that is made up of mistakes without realizing that a whole course correction is needed. Better to be growing in the knowledge of God little by little, **"line upon line, and precept upon precept, here a little, there a little", [Isaiah 28:10]** and making a little progress in learning than to be struggling along in rejection or neglect of "Biblical Correctness" with no knowledge of God and his ways with no progression of life whatsoever, **[Mark 8: 36], "For what shall it profit a man, if he gain the whole world, and lose his own soul"?**

To be a part of the crowd that makes up **[Isaiah 5: 22], "Therefore as the fire devoureth the stubble, and the flame consumeth the chaff, so their root shall be as rottenness, and their blossom shall go up as dust: because they have cast away the law of the Lord of hosts, and despised the word of the Holy One of Israel"**, is to pass an eternal death sentence on yourself and your posterity. **[Deuteronomy 30:19-20], "I call heaven and earth to record this day against you, that I have set before you life and death, blessing and cursing: therefore choose life that both thou and thy seed may live: Vs. 20, That thou mayest love the Lord thy God, and that thou mayest obey his voice, and that thou mayest cleave unto him: for *HE IS THY LIFE and THE LENGTH OF THY DAYS*".**

VIII. INGREDIENTS

Ingredient: something that is a component part or an element contributing to the whole. Now the question arises; what are the ingredients of life; not the existence that man has reduced it to, but life in it's fullness of meaning with the peace, joy, happiness, fulfillment, etc, that God intended all men should enjoy, without which there is no life or significant purpose, resulting in just an everyday drudgery of existence going through the actions of life but never really experiencing it, being as **"whited sepulchers full of dead men's bones"**, **[Matthew23:27]**.'

Let's see if we can identify at least some of the "ingredients" that would contribute to this life wherein man must dwell in order to live and not just maintain an existence where the most cruel, conniving and scheming survive, preying on and exploiting each other and whoever else they can victimize. We have seen examples of that in our world past, and there are some extremely graphic examples still very much in existence today which is likely to continue and intensify unless man's experiences an unexpected enrichment and enhancement in his intelligence level, shall we say a **[Romans 12: 1-2], "with a definite Biblical orientated renewing of the mind",** which to this point is conspicuous by its absence throughout the bulk of humanity. These necessary ingredients for life are basically unknown, thus not experienced or practiced by the vast majority of mankind, and to an embarrassing realization, even lacking to some extent in the Christian community where these things are believed in, though maybe not specifically taught and definitely not emphasized as they should be, but only occasionally alluded to.

This explains the reason why our world and nation is in the horrible condition it is in. This is a result of man's attempts to substitute his own rules, regulations, and laws based on his own ignorance of what is really required of these "necessary ingredients". His feeble attempt without these "ingredients" to create some sort of a semblance of order in his survivalistic existence has failed miserably. What is equally as bad is he doesn't even show the intelligence to realize he has a problem, recognize what his problem is, nor does he exhibit the knowledge or desire to correct it. He speaks of his dilemmas in generalities but without acknowledging his rebellion and disobedience to God's principles as their cause, **[Isaiah 5: 24], "Therefore as the fire devoureth the stubble, and the flame consumeth the chaff, so their root shall be as rottenness, and their blossom shall go up as dust: because they have cast away the law of the Lord of hosts, and despised the word of the Holy One of Israel"**.

The increasing dilemma's are constantly being debated and analyzed hour after hour, day after day, on and on, but with no solutions as yet forthcoming from the minds of the debaters, dialoguers or whoever gets into the fray with their own contribution of idiocy and confusion. The politicians speak of this in the generality of needing a change with no specifics as to what they mean as "change" or directions and instructions to bring about that change. Then we have the pope making the statement, *"our pressing and immediate task is of improving the world in which we live"*. This has always been a pressing, a continuing, and immediate need. You don't have to be a leader of any sort to come to that conclusion, but until you can, and will, outline the specifics and essentials for implementing and accomplishing and this, you fail as a leader.

If we can identify at least some of the things humanity needs to build and enjoy life together without being at each others throats, then maybe we can understand why we need the essentials of that life as outlined and taught only in God's Word of Truth. These must be seen as "needs" that bring security and calmness to the heart, renewal to the mind, and prosperity to the soul, thus the nation; not just "wants" that cater to the fickle emotions and feelings of the selfish, greedy undisciplined mentality. It is absolutely essential that we each learn and know **"how to possess our vessels with honour", [1 Thessalonians 4: 4],** and know how to make the distinction, and determine the value between the two, what we really need, versus what we think we need, our wants that have a real tendency to control our lives.

The needs required for life must occupy our thoughts or we will fail to pursue and provide them, thus an existence is what we misinterpret as life and settle for. It is because of this that humanity wastes their lives and vitality pursuing wants of the "if it feels good, do it" mentality that only demand more but never satisfy the longing of the soul for fulfillment. Thus the lives and years are totally wasted; occasionally enjoyed in a worldly sense of fun and pleasure by a few, but nevertheless for the purposes God intended, wasted. This perverted level of mentality is passed on to the young, and the cycle continues on to their offspring of following generations for their gradual, certain, and eventual destruction. **[Deuteronomy 30: 19], "I call heaven and earth to record this day against you, that I have set before you life and death, blessing and cursing: therefore choose life that *both thou and thy seed may live.***

Now to some ingredients! Love; a very basic need, but where did this idea come from as to its application and need to supply harmonious caring and sharing among people? Is this an exterior idea that man invented that he learned to initiate by trial and error? He hasn't really seemed to have learned much about it, its demands and reason for it, its use, its beneficial rewards, and administration, as he needs to learn and apply in order to bring about its results throughout his species. So we continue to war within and among ourselves. The tragic consequence is that instead of a nation where people contribute to the enrichment of each others life, they develop animosity and jealousy etc, etc, and etc, **biting and devouring with the tongue** by words that tend to discouragement and death rather than encouragement and life, **[Galatians 5: 15]**. Man has initiated some exterior laws in a bungling attempt to stop this but has failed terribly in this area also. All he has accomplished is the building of more detention centers and prisons to separate his failures from the rest of society. He hasn't been able to **induce a change in the heart** so these offensive things won't happen to begin with, so the transgressions and wars continue.

There is much more that could be said and written about the subject of "love" and its demands and what they by necessity must be to be affective and produce a viable successful society, culture, and nation. *Love for God and his righteousness must be the top priority.* We can say we love God and one another, but if our allegiance is not to God's teaching and examples of righteousness and holiness exhibited through our Lord and Saviour Jesus Christ, then we become negligent in our pursuit of these necessary ingredients of life and life more abundantly and suffer the consequences, proving ourselves to be charlatans in our claims. This leads to the condition of the nation we have today. Additional thought, study, and meditation will be left up to the readers and hope they will pursue it for their own good as well as the ones they will affect through their relationships. What radiates out from you is the fallout those around you will experience and be subjected to, and you are responsible for that fallout, whether it be good or evil.

Longsuffering or patience: endurance of an offense is definitely an ingredient of life and the pursuit of happiness. This is a characteristic of life that is sadly lacking in humanity, being quite difficult for most of us to manifest on a consistent basis, especially for an offense committed against us or a person close to us. Patience is neither easy to come by nor to maintain, and the lack of it has caused innumerable conflicts and problems. One of the reasons for this is the absence of another absolutely essential ingredient for peace among us: FORGIVENESS. Try that one on for size and see how it fits, or simply APOLOGIZING and asking for forgiveness for an offense committed, or maybe a simple misunderstanding where there was no offense, but for the sake of peace and need for unity, an apology was offered anyhow.

Mans stupidity of pride quite often prevents this with continuing disastrous results. Here is a whole new area many people never get control of; consequently they never experience the benefits and far reaching positive results and rewards that it can produce. There is to much emphasis put on seeking revenge, getting even, rather than **"initiating peace and doing always those things that please God", [John 8:29].** I have heard it said that, "the only person you should ever get even with is the person who does you good". People that exist with spiteful, hateful, antagonistic attitudes as a way and condition of life will pass these destructive traits on to their children. This will happen as a normal progression, or digression, as the basic sinful nature the children were born with naturally flows in this direction, and without correction will continue on to the succeeding generations, expanding and intensifying as it goes. So we see grandparents today raising their grandchildren because they never exerted the intelligence, time, effort, and energy to correct this downward spiral of incompetence and irresponsibility in their own children. This may be due to the fact it was not corrected in them when they were children.

Every since our governing officials decided to remove and excommunicate God and his Biblical influence and direction from the public forum, this condition has been escalating at an alarming rate and leaving multitudes of destroyed lives and souls in its wake. **[Hosea 4:6-7], "My people are destroyed for lack of knowledge: because thou hast rejected knowledge, I will also reject thee, that thou shalt be no priest to me: seeing thou hast forgotten the law "Word" of thy God, I will also forget thy children. As they were increased, so they sinned against me: therefore I will change their glory into shame".**

Are you enjoying the curse of shame we as Americans have brought on ourselves with our "leaders", our own countrymen, squabbling among themselves blaming each other for America's dilemma's she is currently burdened with and the general population lacking the wherewithal to call them to account and initiate a positive God oriented change? And not a one of them has a viable answer for the solution to these ever mounting problems. **God is still waiting in his place, [Hosea 5: 15], "for our acknowledging of our offenses and seeking his face"!**

Maybe we have not as yet suffered enough afflictions to wake us up to the realization that longer we **"continue to think as we have always thought we will continue to get what we have always got".** It is long overdue for America to arise to a **[Romans 12: 2] Biblical renewing of her wretched mind set and initiating [2 Corinthians 10: 5], "Casting down imaginations, and every high,** and low, **thing that exalts itself against the knowledge of God , and bringing every thought into the captivity of Christ.** It is this desperately needed "knowledge of God" that will prevent the **"destruction" of [Hosea 4:6]** that encompasses men as individuals and nations of multitudes.

Gentleness: Probably most often seen in the bonding of a mother and child but just recently observed between a young father and his little daughter that was quite impressive. This beautiful situation was encouraging, comforting, and touching. Scenes such as this give evidence of that which is possible and should be more in evidence in our species. This is in many cases and in many countries non-existent. It is a characteristic of a real inner strength that many in their erroneous mentalities concerning being real men consider as a sign of weakness. But then those that try to maintain this sort of erroneous mentality are wrong about a great many things but lack the knowledge and understanding to know it, the strength and courage to admit it, and the wisdom and intelligence to correct them.

Good manners including pleasant language and conduct: is an area of training that is vital to good wholesome relationships with all, whether or not we ever come into contact with them, but is essential to our own self development and character of value and worth to the world and society we live in. It is good to pass this kind of character and attitude on to our children for them to enjoy the benefits of life and be appreciated by those around them. This may become more difficult under the present humanistic constitutional rights demanded, as one person's rights collide with another person demanding their rights heading in a different direction. Whose rights are to prevail, and what guidelines do we have for making that determination? If traffic control devices are essential to providing safe orderly conditions on the streets and byways, aren't there some spiritual, psychological traffic control elements needed to provide and maintain a decent, orderly, safe, progression of life among the people that will insure harmonious togetherness, **[Ephesians 2: 4-7]**, that intelligent people would be willing to abide by? Come to think of it, the intelligent ones do!

Without these things in place, in this time of relativity, who is to say what manners are good and which are not, especially if I have my rights to conduct myself according to my own rules, which must be by definition as good as, and equal to your rules, or maybe even better, depending on my mood at the time. Without any spiritual, intelligent, psychological traffic lights in place to determine order within the intersections and along the broad way of existence; might becomes right, and relativity doesn't even matter. It becomes a survival of the biggest, cruelest, meanest, or the conniving, scheming ones among society who are able to impose their self proclaimed rights upon the smaller, weaker ones. Thus the whole society becomes a mass of chaos and confusion with the imposition of rights, whether right or wrong, but who's to say, controlled by the most able or ruthless regardless of whether they are right or wrong. Might, even in its most subtle forms, becomes a forced right, and chaos, confusion and calamity continue to reign totally without reason or purpose other than self exaltation and exercising of control over others. This looks alarmingly like the world we are living, or existing, in today

Let's bring in caring, courtesy, consideration, and kindness as contributors to this thing we call life as opposed to rudeness, indifference, selfishness, etc, which reduces the whole thing to a condition of survivalistic existence. This is where the majority of the world it seems has been for ages, and judging from the world wide atrocities and idiocy that prevails and is on the increase, is where the world and our America is at today and will continue with her present prevailing low level of mentality. There must be something within the present day mentality that initiated this destructive condition and maintains it. There are however, many that seem to be of a totally different mindset that prefer to embrace and practice the ingredients of life that produce such things as happiness, peace, and joy; the things that strengthen, enrich and enhance life rather than break it down and destroy it. I have been acquainted with people of both camps and by far prefer the people who tend to add to the construction of life rather than its destruction by biting and devouring one another with their tongue, the results of sick minds. **[Galatians 5: 15]**.

Those of the constructive camp learn about, pursue, and contribute of the life giving attributes that encourage and assist each other in their day to day living while those of the destructive mindset only detract and discourage with no hope or peace of mind. Let's see if we can find a few more of these life giving ingredients. It is interesting to realize that we as individuals can accumulate these things and share their life giving qualities with others. This brings to mind the idea of Biblical math. We can add to and multiply blessings,**[Proverbs 25: 11], [2 Peter 1:2],** or we can take away, subtract blessings from others with a devouring tongue. There is a whole study in this area as to Biblical analogies that are quite interesting, enlightening, and encouraging that I intend to pursue as I proceed through life.

Let's try "goodness" on for size and see if it fits as desirable, needed, conducive and contributive to life. Is it something that we need to see more among us that has a positive affect on our society and culture including myself? If so, then maybe it is of great enough value for me to investigate and incorporate into my own life for the benefit of others as well as myself, being one of those things that enriches our marriages and **"accompany salvation", [Hebrews 6:9, and "always please God", [John 8: 29]**.

Goodness is defined as, "excellence, and virtue", two qualities that are desperately needed in today's America that have been on the wane for the last several decades and in some areas are completely absent. We see evidence of this in many of out educational systems and facilities where excellence and virtue have been replaced with absolute garbage and filth, deception and outright character destroying nonsense. It is amazing, given the fact that these people are required to be somewhat educated, they still don't seem to exhibit the common sense and intelligence to realize there are correct, positive things that need to be taught to these young minds that will contribute to their character building attributes that are vitally essential for their over all success in life. It certainly places the character of ones promoting these things in question, regardless of their "so called" educational credentials".

We have heard no end from the experts that what we need is more education. Maybe more of "better education" based on Biblical standards and values is what is really needed. Instead, in spite of the millions of dollars poured into it, the standards have been consistently lowered with the natural results of "dumbing down" following close behind. So much for higher education as it is practiced today! I have no problem with better education, but the term "better education" from a worldly standpoint is a relative term, the defining of which has been primarily left up to total incompetents, resulting in our young people being indoctrinated firmly and deeply into the "if it feels good, do it" philosophy of our present day system and culture. There are exceptions; no thanks to the state educational system and authorities with the rules and regulations they have forced into being that have given them ultimate control over the children and the educational input they are to receive to influence and shape their young minds.

In spite of all this we still have a number of young people that turn out quite well for which we can be very thankful. Regardless, we still have many young people slipping through the cracks as to the academic necessities and needed requirements they will need to be mentally, spiritually, and psychologically equipped to meet the real world.

When our young people need to learn the general and specifics of reading, writing, mathematics, etc, etc, to meet the requirements of an ever demanding world, why are they forced to waste time while some incompetent, by law, tries to convince them that they evolved from some piece of slime out of the ocean billions of years ago and that they themselves are nothing but some higher form of animal? Yet they don't even approach the history of our nation so our young people have a thorough knowledge and understanding of their national heritage, how their nation came to be, it's foundational structure, and its purpose, with the hopes and dreams contained therein that are theirs.

Throughout the last one-hundred,-two-hundred years, the ones responsible for the safe guarding of the nation have increasingly suffered a mental lapse of judgment in their responsibilities to the nation and her people. So here we are; a nation where relativity has blurred the difference between right and wrong and good and bad to the point where it is difficult to comprehend and establish a difference. With no absolutes for guidance and direction, there's no use for correction because everything is relative, so there is really no purpose for being. Well has Shakespeare said, and with emphasis, **"What fools ye mortals be"** and with the present prevailing level of mentality, it is due to get much worse before it gets better. With no acknowledgement of transgressions and no corrective authority or measures intelligently at work, no one accountable, no responsibility, and no one to answer to, where do we go from here. With no direction, no correction, and no desire or will to have any, we as a nation have lost our way. With God and his guidance and counsel excommunicated, we have no purpose or reason for being. Indeed, what is there left to hope for? **BUT GOD [Ephesians 2: 4]!**

There are many other things that could be included as ingredients for life which enrich, beautify it, making it productive and enjoyable, but they all must contribute to a purpose extending beyond our "flash in the pan" period of time on this earth. If the only reason for man's existence is to pay taxes to a corrupt state entity created by man, then human existence is nothing but an exercise of futility. Is that the sole purpose of the existence of the state, to collect taxes and spend them however they see fit without any accountability from anyone? I have to believe that a human life was meant for much greater things than existing to pay taxes for whatever deviously imposed state entity was collecting them. Surely God had greater purposes in mind for his creation when he created it, and them.

There has to be a much larger scope of meaning to life than puny man is able to give to it on his own with his exhibited limited intelligence while fulfilling his purpose as a taxpayer. Life must have more meaning than that or it has no worthwhile purpose. To enjoy a few things, struggle through the heartaches and miseries, eat, sleep, work and die does not seem sufficient for all that is involved in a lifespan. There must be more, much more than man has been able to provide for himself, and intelligent people will demand and seek it. There has to be realms of reality beyond the claims of the secular humanist, the atheist, the evolutionist, and all the other worldly minded anti-God elements struggling through their allotted time here on earth to end up, where!

It is hard to understand why anyone with even a little intelligence would throw in with a group that has such a loser mentality. Maintaining a position of absolutely no hope of anything beyond were they are with no benefits provided in that position and choosing to remain there is absolutely amazing in its magnitude of idiocy and ignorance. It certainly gives reason to question the sanity of these people and being declared innocent by reason of insanity doesn't fit here. On the contrary, they are guilty by reason of insanity when the solution to their insanity is available and rests on a simple choice. Are they really to insane to make a choice to receive life and blessing instead of remaining in a continuing condition of death and cursing?

Indeed, one of the main ingredients to life is the developed ability to make good choices, and then exercising that ability for choices that need to be made every day on a 24/7 basis. I use the term "developed ability" here because we all have abilities to greatness that lay undeveloped with in us because they are undiscovered, unrealized, unacknowledged, unknown, and thus, untaught, and so remain "undeveloped" and so unused and dead, waiting for a sane decision to bring them to life. The world is full of psychologically, emotionally, blinded people who struggle thru an existence led, or driven, by other psychologically, emotionally, blinded people who themselves are void of the realization and benefits of the ingredients of life. Consequently their whole existence is an existence of denial of the life that awaits them. It has become a world of existence and cursing versus a realm of life and blessing, and the only thing that separates them is intelligent choice. Indeed it has been so for millennia, and is still a warfare; a warfare of; which choice do I make next. Do I make a sane choice, one that gives peace, joy, and life; or remain with an insane condition; one that experience has shown me will bring additional, confusion, turmoil, heartache, misery, death, and curses that I must endure constantly.

It kind of reminds me of the dude in a commercial on television that is "in debt up to his eyeballs" crying, "won't somebody please help me" when intelligent choices would have prevented his plight to begin with. But this thing of intelligence, sometimes referred to as wisdom, or used in conjunction with wisdom, another extremely important ingredient of life, seems to be in very short supply throughout humanity, including the land of the free, and the home of the brave. This void has been a part of man every since he has existed. It seems as though man and problems are synonymous, they go together somewhat like the proverbial horse and carriage. **[Job 5:7], "Yet man is born unto trouble as the sparks fly upward".**

If someone else doesn't create problems for him, he will invariably create his own, and in creating his own, he creates and imposes them on others, being especially and adversely affective on those closest to them; loved ones and family members. I believe this is referred to as "self destructing" and manifests itself in, once again, the choices we make, or fail to make, whichever the case may be. If we choose the wrong frame of mind, the wrong attitude, we create problems, wrong thoughts create wrong ways and conduct; result, more problems. **[Isaiah 55: 8-9], "For my thoughts are not your thoughts, neither are your ways my ways, saith the Lord. For as the heavens are higher than the earth, so are my ways higher than your ways, and my thoughts than your thoughts".** Mankind has a difficult time learning even simple lessons. May God have mercy on his stupid, rebellious creation.

And so he struggles on, filling his own life, societies, cultures, and world with additional dilemma's and problems he doesn't have the intelligence to solve, nor the intelligence to prevent in the first place. It seems as though he has a natural inclination to the ingredients of death and cursing, but has great difficulty making choices that reward him with life and blessing and then following through on them to the benefit of himself and his fellow man. So man continues to take his lumps but never learns how to avoid them, or at least learn from them. Once again I cannot help but remember our old friend Shakespeare's words, **"What fools ye mortals be"**.

Little did he realize the gravity of that statement as proven in our modern and post-modern world, America definitely included! It seems we have gone out of our way to create and invent new ways to be fools, new ways to bring curses on our selves, our children, and our nation. There are, however, exceptions to this for which we can be very thankful. But then who are we to thank for these exceptions but God. All man has done is create additional problems for himself and his fellow man, and has not proven himself thank worthy except in some very minor exchange of niceties which get lost in the mass of confusion and chaos he has heaped on himself and each other.

Any fool or group of fools can cause problems and create dilemmas, but it is going to take more intelligence than man has exhibited thus far to solve them. To walk softly and carry a big stick is wisdom, but when you have bound yourself up with incompetence to the point you can't even recognize what that stick, or sword, consists of or use it as necessary, it becomes useless and overbearing to carry. And after awhile; the resultant relaxation of vigilance will prove your undoing. So we find WISDOM and VIGILANCE together as necessary ingredients for life, blessing, and preservation along with a multitude of other necessities, some of which have been mentioned here. This is by no means a complete list which needs to be explored, considered, and studied with the application of DILIGENCE. Diligence in pursuit of what! Man in all his combined secularism, atheism, humanism, evolution, relativity, etc, has not provided, and indeed cannot provide a sufficient answer for that, for they have none, **BUT GOD!**

NOTES

NOTES

NOTES

NOTES

NOTES

www.ingramcontent.com/pod-product-compliance
Lightning Source LLC
LaVergne TN
LVHW011713060526
838200LV00051B/2889